nora's di

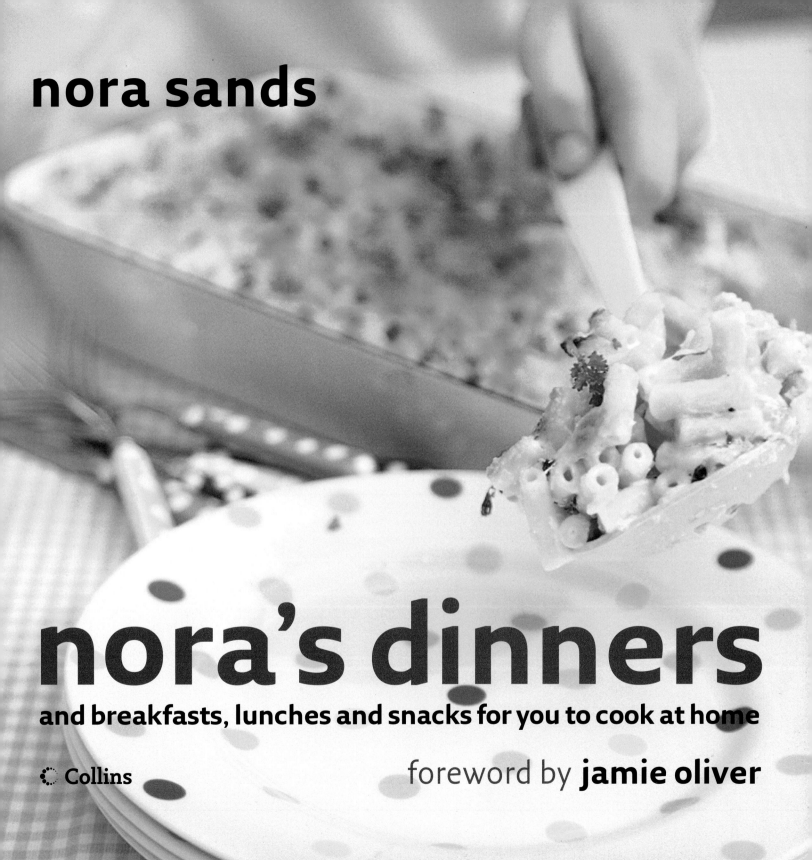

nora sands

nora's dinners

and breakfasts, lunches and snacks for you to cook at home

Collins

foreword by **jamie oliver**

First published in 2006 by
Collins, an imprint of
HarperCollinsPublishers
77–85 Fulham Palace Road
Hammersmith, London W6 8JB

The Collins website address is:
www.collins.co.uk

09 08 07 06
6 5 4 3 2 1

A catalogue record for this book is available from the British Library

Photographer: Véronique Leplat
Food and Props Stylist: Felicity Barnum-Bobb
Designers: Valerie Fong, Richard Marston
Editor: Gillian Haslam
Proofreader: Kate Parker
Indexer: Hilary Bird

ISBN 13:978-0-00-720661-2
ISBN 10:0-00-720661-5

Colour reproduction by Colourscan, Singapore
Printed and bound by Printing Express Ltd, Hong Kong

contents

jamie's foreword

Last year Nora Sands, a dinner lady from Kidbrooke School in Greenwich, became my most powerful ally in the school dinners campaign, where we succeeded in getting the Government to undertake a massive U-turn on their social and nutritional policies for the kids in British schools. We're hopeful that this will benefit children for years to come. I can honestly say that without Nora I would never have been able to achieve my goal for the 'Feed Me Better' campaign in my television documentary *Jamie's School Dinners*. Even though she was a dinner lady of tremendous efficiency and integrity, like many other dinner ladies, she only had the option to cook or reheat food from the menus provided to her. When Greenwich Council very bravely allowed me into Nora's School, I only dreamed about the kind of radical transformation that she pushed forward and, to this day, her kitchen and meals still stand as a wonderful example of what can be achieved.

When it comes to Nora, I'm going to tell it like it is! She is the only woman in the world, apart from my wife, who makes me jump to attention when she needs something or wants something done. When she wants to make sure I'm paying attention to her, she whacks me on the arms until I'm black and blue, whilst emphasizing every other syllable. When working with her in the school kitchens she would eratically shriek various commands and information at me so very loudly that I was constantly on edge!

But, as her lovely husband said to me when I first met him, when it comes to Nora you either love her or hate her. And nearly everyone I know just loves her. If they don't, it's because they just don't know her well enough yet because, and I sincerely mean this, she is one of life's special people. And I don't say that lightly (I also know that she's going to hate me for saying this and she'll be calling me a 'silly eejit'). She really is the most painfully honest person that I have ever met. She has a heart of gold and moral standards to die for. I know that if I was to introduce her to the Queen or a local councillor or a random celebrity that she would speak to them as she does to anyone she meets – plain and simple. Her honesty and experience can be seen very clearly in this book, with her helpful tips and short cuts, the nutritional information and wonderful photographs. And, of course, all her simple, modern-day, great British classic recipes. I know that families will love this cookbook as the recipes can be made with your kids of any age.

Nora, I know in your wildest dreams you never thought you would write a cookbook. All I want to say is that you deserve it and it's really great. Well done!

Jamie

love Jamie 'Black and Blue' Oliver
xxxxxxxxxxxx

nora's introduction

I have loved cooking ever since I was a little girl. My mum used to grow her own vegetables and she taught me all about fresh vegetables, fruit, meat and fish. We would go to the garden, dig the vegetables up and she would let me help her prepare our family meals. I loved learning all her little cooking secrets, and our time together in the kitchen made us very close. It was always so much fun spending time cooking with her, but it was even more of a riot when the whole family got together to eat and laugh and argue over who got the biggest portions!

It's not always easy for busy mums and dads to find the time to cook meals – I know, I have two kids of my own. But it makes me sad that some children don't know anything at all about cooking fresh food, or think that chicken only comes in funny shapes. If you watched *Jamie's School Dinners*, you'll know what I'm talking about. Now, I'll be the first to admit that I don't know much about posh ingredients, let alone how to pronounce them (celeriac, ciabatta, mozzarella to name a few), but I've seen so many kids who don't even know a carrot from a potato. And that really worries me.

I've met so many children whose only experience in the kitchen is warming up ready meals in the microwave. So, I decided to write this book to get kids excited about cooking, and to share my experiences and favourite family recipes. I'm not a chef and would never pretend to be so. This is simple home cooking for kids to try, and not complicated, fancy restaurant food. And if anyone tries to tell you that home-cooked food can't be delicious too, they'll have to answer to me.

You'll find my recipes really easy to follow, I can promise you that. There are lots of recipes that are so simple even the youngest members of your family can have a turn in the kitchen, like Banana Toast on page 50. Some are a bit more difficult, such as Mum's Best Sunday Roast on page 106, and might need a little help from an adult or an older brother or sister – but getting everyone in the kitchen making things together is half the fun!

If you have a sweet-tooth, you'll probably want to turn straight to the cakes and desserts section. I dare you not to love the Choca-Block on page 118. But I really want you to try making all the other meals as well. If you've never cooked dinner before, don't worry, try making the Monsterella Pizza on page 70. It's super easy, and you'll never want to order a take-away again!

I bet you thought that pick 'n' mix was only for sweets. If you are afraid of trying new ingredients then these sections are perfect for you. You can try Pick 'n' Mix Perfect Pasta on page 80 or Super Salad on page 60, and come up with your own custom recipes on your first try!

I don't expect you to be able to do everything, but if you are able to cook just one thing at the weekend it would be great. If I can do it, anyone can give it a go! So get into the kitchen with your family and friends and have fun!

Nora Sands.

I've found the kitchen, now what?

The first rule is that you should always make sure there is an adult around before you start to cook. Some recipes need adult supervision, and some just need a bit of help from an adult or older brother or sister to lift hot, heavy pots or to cut fiddly fruit. You must promise always to ask permission before you turn on the oven or hob.

Next, you need to decide what you want to cook! Look at the contents page and decide what meal you would like to cook for - breakfast or maybe lunch - then see what takes your fancy from the list of recipes in that chapter. Be sure to read the whole recipe all the way through. That way, you'll know exactly what ingredients and equipment you'll need, and you'll be ready for each step. Even if you don't understand the steps at first, you should still take the time to read the whole recipe. It will all make sense once you start cooking.

You'll need to clear and clean some space in your kitchen so that you have plenty of room. Gather all your equipment together, and then start to get your ingredients ready. Cooking is so much easier if you're all prepared before you begin!

Each recipe has a list of equipment that you will need and a list of ingredients needed to make the recipe. It also has the symbols shown below which tell you how many minutes it will take you to **prepare** your ingredients and how many minutes it will take you to cook the recipe.

prep cook

5 25

Where there is a '0' in the symbol, it means there is no cooking to be done! Each recipe is divided into steps to make it easy to follow.

get to know your tools

You don't need to have fancy electric gizmos to be able to cook great food. My mum certainly didn't, and I'm convinced she was the best cook in the world. These are some of the basic things you'll need, most of which you'll probably already have in the kitchen. And for those things you might not have, I've given some suggestions for something similar. For example, if you don't have a pestle and mortar, you can use a bowl and the end of a rolling pin.

baking tray – these are flat and are used for baking things in the oven like cookies and pizzas.

chopping board – whenever you cut food you should use a chopping board to protect your table or kitchen worktop. You should never cut raw meat on the same board you are using for cutting vegetables, so try to have different chopping boards for raw meat, cooked meat and vegetables. If you only have one board, cut all your vegetables first, and be sure to clean the board with hot soapy water after cutting meat.

colander – this is a special bowl with holes for draining cooked food like potatoes or pasta, or for rinsing fruit or vegetables.

frying pan – this is good for cooking food on the hob that doesn't need any extra liquid, such as eggs, sausages or chopped vegetables. Non-stick pans are really easy to wash up, but be careful not to use metal tools in them or you'll scrape the special coating off. If you don't have non-stick, you may need a little extra butter or oil to keep food from sticking.

garlic press – this is great for getting peeled garlic mashed up quickly, but if you don't have one you can always use a knife to chop your garlic into tiny bits.

grater – this is usually a metal box with a handle on top, with sharp holes of different sizes on each side. It is used for grating cheese or vegetables such as carrots, but is also used for scraping the skin off lemons or oranges (the skin is called the zest).

hand blender and food processor – I know I said you don't need electric gadgets in your kitchen, but if you're lucky enough to have these they are great time savers. Food processors have attachments that will make fast work of chopping, mixing, and grating. A hand blender can be used straight in your pan or bowl. Both gadgets have really sharp parts and you need to use them carefully, so do not ever use them unless an adult is around and be sure they show you exactly how to use them safely.

knives – knives are probably the most important part of your kitchen kit, but you don't need a great big set. You'll need a small or medium sharp knife for cutting veggies or fruit. You may need a slightly bigger sharp knife for cutting meat. I'm sure you don't need me to tell you that you should be very, very careful using sharp knives (or sharp anything, really). If you need help from an adult, you must always ask.

ladle – this is like a big spoon on a long handle used for scooping up soup or sauce out of a pot or bowl.

measuring jug –this is a special jug that has lines and measurements on it so that you know how much liquid you need. They are really handy for making stock from stock cubes.

measuring spoons – these aren't totally necessary, but they are really useful. Each spoon has its size written on it like 1 teaspoon (1 tsp), 1 tablespoon (1 tbsp). If you don't have them, you can use a large eating spoon to measure a table spoon (make sure you heap up the ingredient on the spoon so it's a nice big spoonful), and a teaspoon for a teaspoon!

mixing bowls – these are much larger than cereal or soup bowls and are used for mixing up ingredients, such as batters or dough, or for large amounts of dry ingredients, like Morning Munch on page 48. Be sure to read your recipe first to make sure you pick the right size bowl before you add your ingredients.

muffin tins – these are special trays with dents in them. You can slot paper cases into the dents and pour muffin batter into them.

oven gloves – these are special padded mittens made especially to protect your hands when you are putting things into or taking things out of a hot oven. If you don't have oven gloves, you may have something similar or can use folded tea towels (they must not be damp though as you might burn yourself), but always get an adult to give you a hand or supervise when working with a hot oven. Do not use your winter mittens!

oven-proof dishes – these are usually made out of glass or ceramic and are safe to go into a hot oven. Be sure to check with an adult before putting any dish into the oven, because if you use the wrong kind it can break.

pestle and mortar –this is usually made out of stone, granite, ceramic or sometimes wood. It looks like a small heavy bowl with a fat stick inside, and is used for grinding up things like seeds. The stone or granite ones are the heaviest so do the best job, but if you don't have one, you can use a bowl and the end of a rolling pin.

potato masher – a good, old-fashioned stainless steel masher is the best option. If you don't have one, you can use the back of a ladle or a large fork.

pots/saucepans – these have higher sides than frying pans and usually come with lids. They are good for cooking things in larger quantities, or for liquidy foods such as soups or sauces, or for boiling water to cook potatoes or pasta. The lids help to keep the liquid from evaporating when cooking, or help things to cook a little faster.

roasting tins – these have higher sides than baking trays, and are used for cooking larger things in the oven, such as chicken, or if you have a lot of cut-up veggies to roast.

rolling pin – this is a long and heavy round bar used for flattening out dough. They're usually made out of wood, but you might have one made out of metal, ceramic or stone.

salad spinner – this is like a large plastic bowl with an inner layer, plus a lid with a handle on it. You simply put your washed lettuce leaves inside it, put on the lid and turn the handle. This spins the inside of the bowl, so all the water drips off the lettuce leaves. Very clever!

sieve – this is similar to a colander, but it has much, much smaller holes. It's also good for rinsing or draining things, but since the holes are smaller you can use it for rice or other food with tiny bits that might slip through the holes of a colander. You will also use a sieve to help get smoother sauces or soups by draining the liquid through so you can get rid of seeds or lumps or other things you want to get out. You will also use a sieve when you are baking, to help add air to the flour before you add liquid. You'll learn more about this when you are making Caramel Apple Pancakes on page 42 or Choca-Block on page 118.

spatula – there are two kinds. The first has a flat surface attached to a long handle, and it is used to turn things over like pancakes, or for lifting hot things out of a pan. The second kind is flexible and made out of rubber or soft plastic and is great for scraping out bowls. They're sometimes called scrapers.

timer – this is sort of like a clock, but it counts down how many minutes your food needs to cook. You can also use a normal clock by checking the time and adding on the minutes until your dish is ready, but kitchen timers are really helpful if you have a few things on the go! They 'ping' when the time is up – very useful!

tin opener – does what it says to the tin.

tongs – these are great if you have them. They're made for grabbing or turning hot food, such as sausages or chicken parts. They're really handy for everything, including a barbeque!

vegetable peeler – this makes fast work of peeling potatoes or carrots. Always remember to use the peeler away from your body: never peel towards you. You should get an adult to show you how, and if you are having trouble get them to help you (so that you don't cut yourself).

weighing scales – these are special scales used in the kitchen (the ones you use in the bathroom are too big and won't have the right measurements). They are important for getting the amounts of your ingredients just right when you really need them to be exact, like when you are baking. Electric scales are very accurate, or use traditional scales with a needle that points at the weight. If you don't have scales, get an adult to help you work out how much you will need from the weight on the side of the packet. But remember, if you don't get your measurements right in the first instance, you won't get the result you expect!

whisk – this is a long handle with metal loops attached, and is used for mixing things like eggs or batter. The loops help get some air into the mixture, and you'll see little bubbles form in your mixture. You can also get electric whisks, which are very handy for mixing batter quickly, but do not use an electric whisk without adult supervision, and be sure they show you how to use it safely.

wok – this is a special large round-bottomed pan used for cooking Asian foods like stir-fry. If you don't have one you can use a large frying pan.

wooden spoons – these are great for stirring anything you are cooking on the hob, and are safe to use on non-stick pans.

top tips for food safety

1. take chilled and frozen food home quickly

then put it in your fridge or freezer as soon as you can. Cold or frozen foods shouldn't become warm as that's when bad bacteria start to grow very quickly. These bacteria can give you food poisoning.

2. always wash your vegetables

before you cook with them.

3. prepare and store raw and cooked food separately

Keep raw meat and fish at the bottom of your fridge – you mustn't let any juices from the raw meat drip onto other food in your fridge as the juices may contain bad bacteria, which could be dangerous.

4. keep the coldest part of your fridge at 0-5°C

At this temperature the bad bacteria can't grow.

5. check 'use-by' dates

Look for the 'use-by' date on packets of food. You must eat food by this date.

6. keep pets away from food, dishes and worktops

Pets can carry germs and bacteria so you need to keep them well away from your food, the areas where you prepare your food and the dishes you eat your food from.

7. wash your hands thoroughly

You must always wash your hands well:
- before preparing food
- after going to the toilet
- after touching pets
- between working with raw and cooked food

Otherwise you could move germs from your hands onto your food and then into your stomach.

8. keep your kitchen clean

Wash your worktops and utensils – especially between handling food which is to be cooked and raw food.

9. cook food well

If you re-heat food, make sure it's piping hot all the way through so you kill any bad bacteria that may be hanging about.

10. keep hot foods hot and cold foods cold

Don't leave foods standing around as bacteria will grow. If food is meant to be cold, put it in the fridge. If it is meant to be hot, eat it while it is still hot. If you have cooked something and want to save it to eat the next day, you can leave it out until it cools down (keep it covered so flies can't get to it) and then put it in the fridge until you are ready to eat it the next day. Then make sure it is very hot when you heat it up.

wash your hands thoroughly

techniques

These are the basic cooking techniques we use in the recipes that follow. They're really all quite simple and easy to learn.

grinding

You often need to grind up herbs and spices. The best thing to use is a pestle and mortar (see page 14 for description) but you can use a bowl as the mortar and the end of a rolling pin as the pestle as well. Put the things you need to grind in the mortar or bowl, then use the pestle or rolling pin to bash and roll the food until it gets mixed or turns into powder.

stoning fruit

To remove the stone from fruit, cut the fruit in half. Hold one half in one hand and a spoon in the other. Push the spoon under the stone and run the spoon around the stone to loosen it – you may need to give it one last flick to get it out .

sifting

The thing you sift most often is flour or icing sugar. Hold the sieve over a bowl and pour the flour or icing sugar into the sieve. Gently shake or tap the sieve, or stir in small circles with a spoon until all the powder has fallen through the sieve.

chopping

Always use a sharp knife. Make sure an adult sharpens it for you. Try to keep the tip of the knife on your board and use it in a rocking motion. Keep your fingers well away – bend your knuckles towards the blade to protect your fingertips, like you see in this picture.

beating

You can beat anything fairly well to get it creamy or break it up. Don't worry – just go for it, even with eggs. You can use a spoon or an electric whisk, which is shown in this picture.

peeling

Some fruits and vegetables have skins that have to be removed before you eat them because they would be a bit too stringy and tough. When using a peeler, peel away from you until you get used to it, so you don't cut yourself.

grating

You can grate cheese, carrots, apples – anything you like – on a fine setting (the side with the small holes) or coarse setting (the side with the big holes) but be careful not to get your fingers grated! Hand held gaters are particularly good for scraping the skin off citrus fruits. The skin is called the zest.

simmering

For a simmer, turn your heat to its lowest setting. You should only just see the bubbles on the surface of the liquid, showing that it is very nearly getting to the boil. It is a gentle way of cooking something.

boiling

Turn the heat to its highest setting. You should see lots of bubbles in the liquid in the pan.

frying

A heavy non-stick pan is best. Always make sure it's hot before you put anything in – you should hear a sizzle when you put something in. Turn meat every couple of minutes (the heat will seal the edges to keep the juices inside) and turn something delicate like fish at least once during cooking.

roasting

Lots of vegetables are lovely roasted. Have your oven on really high and cover the vegetables with a good coating of olive oil. Try to spoon the hot oil over the food half way through cooking - this is called basting. See page 24 for more instructions on roasting vegetables.

stir-frying

Your pan must be extremely hot so that your ingredients cook through in only a few minutes. Always move the ingredients around with a spoon or spatula. You don't need a wok to stir-fry – a large frying pan will do. Don't put too much in the pan at once - anything not touching the pan is not frying, it's steaming!

mashing

You can use a masher, a fork or the back of a large spoon, but a masher makes life much easier. Whatever you use always make sure you mash well and mash out all the lumps .

weighing and measuring

Make sure you always measure carefully. It will make a difference to your recipe if you get this wrong. To measure liquids, use a measuring jug. To measure butter and dry ingredients, use a weighing scales.

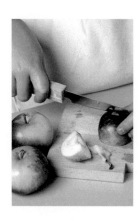

whisking

A whisk should be light and springy. When you whisk, you add air to make your mixture lighter, so hold your bowl and tilt it a bit, then lift the whisk as you use it to stir the mixture very quickly – this will help get lots of air in. If you are whisking to remove lumps, just attack it and give it a good beating!

breaking eggs

Hold the egg in your hand and tap it hard against the edge of a bowl or cup. This should make a crack in the shell and egg white will start to fall out. Quickly put both your thumbs inside the crack and pull the eggshell gently in opposite directions. This will help the egg fall into the bowl or cup.

coring apples

Stand the apple on a board. Put the knife at the top and push down, cutting it in half. Lie each half flat side down and cut in half again. Hold a quarter in one hand and the knife in the other and cut out the core, pulling the knife towards you but only half way. Turn the quarter round and cut from the other end.

draining

The best thing to use is a colander (see page 13). Be careful when draining as you often need to do this when the water is very hot so make sure you wear oven gloves or get an adult to help you. Put the colander in the sink or over a bowl and tip up the saucepan so the water and the food fall into the colander.

eating sensibly

The simple trick to eating healthily is to have a little bit of everything, rather than eating the same things all the time, like having chips every day for lunch! Different foods contain different nutrients – you cannot get everything your body needs to grow and stay healthy from one single food. This does not mean saying goodbye to all your favourite foods and treats, it just means you need to think about how often you eat them, and to be sure to eat a variety of foods.

The chart shows the five main food groups, and how much of the food you eat should be from each group. Most of the food you eat should come from the orange section (bread, other cereals and potatoes), and from the green section (fruit and vegetables) Then come foods from the blue section (milk and dairy foods) and from the red section (meat, fish and other protein) Eat foods from the yellow group (fatty and sugary foods, such as crisps and sweets) – only as a special treat.

So, eat plenty of orange and green, a bit of blue and red and not too much yellow! You don't have to make huge changes to make a difference.

the 5 main food groups

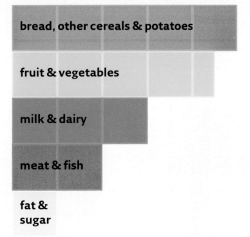

bread, other cereals & potatoes

fruit & vegetables

milk & dairy

meat & fish

fat & sugar

We should all have at least five portions of fruit and vegetables every day.
Here are some easy ways to do this:
- Try swapping a bar of chocolate for a banana as a snack and that's one of your five portions ticked off.
- A bit of salad or some veggies with lunch or dinner and there's a few more ticked.
- A glass of fruit juice or a smoothie is another one ticked!

You should also think about how the foods you are eating are cooked.
Go for boiled potatoes rather than chips so that you are eating less fat. Chips can be an occasional treat.

Treats such as cakes and biscuits certainly aren't banned – I have included some of them in this book for you – it's just best if you don't eat them every day and that you make sure you eat plenty of vegetables and fruit as well.

Drink plenty of water.
It's very easy to get a little bit dehydrated, which means your body doesn't have enough water inside to keep working properly.
- Be sure to have drinks regularly throughout the day, before you really feel thirsty.
- Being dehydrated means you can't concentrate as well, and might have headaches
- Try to drink at least six glasses of liquid every day - more when it is really hot or you have been exercising hard. Fizzy drinks are full of sugar, but fruit juice, milk and water all count!

By cooking your own food and using fresh ingredients you are able to control the things you add, or don't add, and you will make a huge difference to the healthiness of what you eat. And it's just so much more fun – as you're about to find out when you try the recipes in this book.

Always wash your vegetables

make friends with your vegetables

Most vegetables are delicious...it's just a matter of trying them. Be adventurous and try as many different vegetables as you can. See how much colour you can get on your plate. Try The Best Lasagne Ever on page 90 with Quick Carrot Crunch on page 56 and some buttered peas. That way, you have red, orange and green all on your plate at once! Or try adding a Pick 'n' Mix Super Salad on page 60 to your meal, and you can go really crazy with colour.

On the next few pages we mention some of the vegetables that can be found easily in your local supermarket – there are pictures of lots of them on pages 26-7. Now, I know the vegetable aisle may not seem like the most exciting place, but why not try having a treasure hunt to see who can find the strangest sounding, or weirdest looking vegetable?

Some vegetables that you know really well can also come in colours you wouldn't expect, such as purple carrots, orange tomatoes, or pink stripy beans!

Here are some things I've seen at the supermarket. I've not tried all of them yet, but I will once I find the right recipe – just don't ask me to pronounce them!
- **pak choi**
- **celeriac**
- **okra**
- **oyster mushrooms**
- **Jerusalem artichokes**
- **fennel**

Growing up in Ireland, potatoes were a big part of what we ate as a family. There are so many ways of cooking potatoes – not just crisps and chips! Once you've chosen the vegetables you want to try, here are some ways to prepare them.

puréed or mashed – the best vegetables for this are potatoes, butternut squash, carrots, and parsnips. Peel and chop them into big cubes. Cover with cold water, add a good pinch of salt and bring to the boil over a high heat on the hob. Boil for about 15-20 minutes until they are soft (try pushing a knife into a piece – if it goes through to the centre easily, it's probably soft enough). Drain them in a colander using oven gloves and mash with your potato masher or the

puréed or mashed

roasted

boiled

steamed

stir-fried

back of a big spoon. You can blitz in a food processor or you can use a hand blender if you have either one. Add a teaspoon of butter and a bit of salt and pepper. Make sure all the big lumps are mashed out. If you are mashing potatoes and they are a bit lumpy, you can add a big splash of milk to make them smoother. Try putting some herbs, a big spoonful of yoghurt, a teaspoon of mustard, two handfuls of grated cheese or a few shakes of ground nutmeg in your mashed potatoes if you're feeling adventurous!

roasted – roasting is such a nice way to eat vegetables, they taste so good! You can roast pretty much anything, such as tomatoes, mushrooms, onions, carrots, peppers or squash (see the recipe on page 106 for roasting potatoes). Pre-heat your

oven to 200°C/400°F/Gas Mark 6, then chop your veggies into chunks and mix in a bowl with a little olive oil and a pinch of salt and pepper. Throw them into a large roasting tray and, using your oven gloves, place in the hot oven for about 30 minutes. Don't worry if they look a bit burnt around the edges, it all adds to the flavour. Try adding some nice-smelling herbs like rosemary or basil before you cook the veggies.

boiled – this is a really quick way of cooking your vegetables.
potatoes: scrub new potatoes clean – some of the skin can stay on. Peel and cut large potatoes in half. Place in a full saucepan of cold water and add a large pinch of salt. Cover with a lid and bring to the boil over a high heat on the hob. Once they are

boiling, turn the heat down to medium or low and simmer for about 20 minutes or until you can push a knife easily through to the centre. When they are ready, drain them in a colander using your oven gloves. They will be very hot so make sure you ask for help if you need it. Put them in a bowl and sprinkle with a little salt and pepper and add a blob of butter.
other vegetables: Peel and chop the vegetables into small (but not tiny) pieces. Bring a large pan of water to boil over a high heat on the hob, and add a pinch of salt. Throw in the vegetables and when the water starts boiling again, turn the heat down and simmer the vegetables: for green vegetables like peas or broccoli simmer for a few minutes, and for anything else, like carrots, simmer for a little longer. If you are cooking

spinach, this will only take seconds! Be sure not to overcook your vegetables or they will lose their vitamins and lots of flavour. When they are done, they should still be a little bit firm and crunchy. Drain the vegetables in a colander using your oven gloves. Place them in a bowl and add a little oil or butter. For a change, try boiling peas with a herb like mint, or carrots with thyme.

steamed – this is the healthiest way of eating your vegetables. This does not mean it's the most boring! It just means that all of the vitamins aren't washed away by lots of water. You may have a special steamer made out of bamboo or metal, or you can use a colander. Either way, cut your veggies into small pieces and place into your colander or steamer – don't put in too many or else only the ones at the bottom will cook. Place the lid on the steamer and place it snugly over a full pot of water, and then bring to a boil on the hob over a high heat. Cover the colander with a lid from a saucepan. Leave the lid on and steam the veggies for about 20 minutes' depending on how thick they are. Dense veggies such as carrots will take longer to steam than light ones such as courgettes. Like boiling, spinach takes hardly any time at all. You may need to check them every now and then to see if they are ready and to make sure your water hasn't evaporated, but you must get an adult to help you do this since the steam is extremely hot and can easily burn your skin. When the vegetables are ready, put them in a bowl and add a little butter or sprinkle with a little olive oil and lemon juice and add a pinch of salt and pepper if you wish.

stir fried – you can stir-fry just about any vegetable, like peppers, onions, mushrooms or courgettes, but be sure to use slightly more than you think you need because they will get smaller with cooking. Slice your vegetables very thinly. Heat a wok or large frying pan on a high heat then add about 2 tablespoons of olive oil. Throw in your cut vegetables and a pinch of salt and pepper and keep moving them around so they don't stick to the bottom of the pan. Cook until they are a bit soft – it should only take a few minutes. You can keep your stir fry simple and plain or add a few flavours, like coriander, ginger, soy sauce or a bit of chilli. You can also add some cooked chicken, beef, pork or prawns to make it more of a complete meal.

have you seen these vegetables?

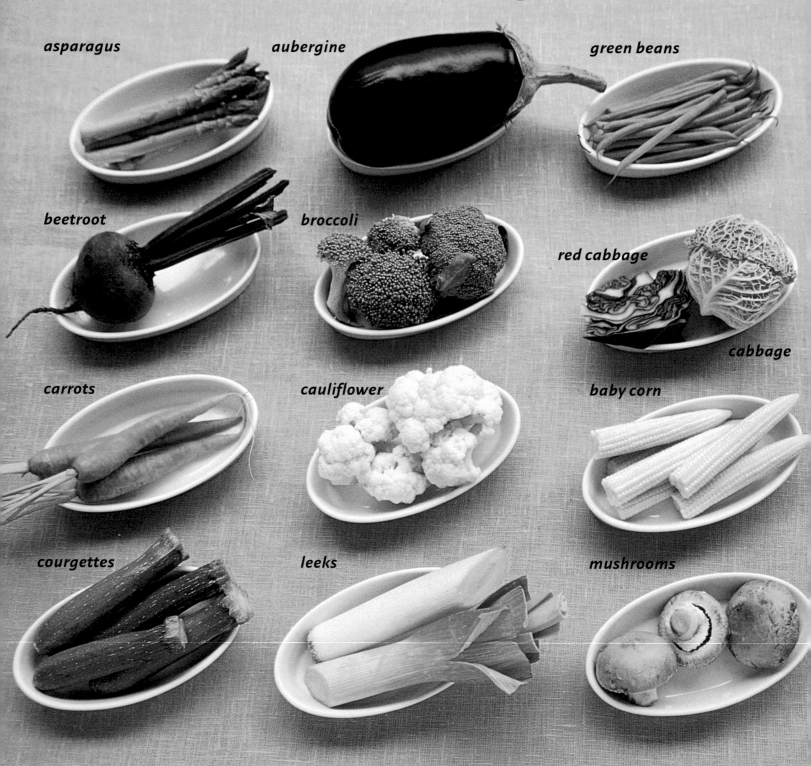

asparagus

aubergine

green beans

beetroot

broccoli

red cabbage

cabbage

carrots

cauliflower

baby corn

courgettes

leeks

mushrooms

parsnip

peas

red pepp

green pepper

red onion

onion

potatoes

baby spinach

spring onions

sweet potato

red tomatoes

multi-coloured tomatoes!

herbs & spices

Don't let the thought of herbs and spices scare you. They add such nice flavour to food, and you probably didn't even realise how many things you probably already eat that are made special by herbs and spices. Did you know that it's coriander that makes curry so nice? And pizza wouldn't be pizza without basil and oregano! And lots of spices are used in puddings and cakes, like cinnamon and nutmeg.

Herbs
Basil – lovely with tomatoes
Coriander
Dill
Mint
Rosemary
Sage
Tarragon
Thyme

Spices
Cinnamon – try it on buttered
   toast
Cumin
Curry powder
Ground chilli
Ground or fresh ginger
Nutmeg

a word on salt and pepper...
Many of my recipes call for a pinch of salt and pepper, because it helps with the flavour. When I say a pinch, I really mean just a pinch. Proper food does not need much salt to make it taste good. You should always taste your food before you serve it, in case you think it needs a little bit more salt and pepper.

fresh chilli   chilli flakes

cinnamon stick

ground coriander

ground cumin

ground cinnamon

chilli powder

cumin seeds

curry paste

fennel seeds

fresh garlic

ground ginger

curry powder

fresh ginger

ground nutmeg

paprika

ground pepper

salt

whole nutmeg

peppercorns

basil

bay

coriander

dill

mint

flat-leaf parsley

curly parsley

rosemary

thyme

Setting the Table

After you've gone to all the trouble of cooking a meal or a snack for your family or friends, it is much nicer if you set the table so you can all eat together. Everyone will appreciate your effort and it gives you a good chance to sit down and have a chat – do you know how your brothers and sisters are doing in school, or what your friend did last weekend? We always ate together as a family and always ended up having a great laugh!

how to set the table

This is one way to set the table. If you don't have a tablecloth or napkins, you can improvise with placemats and kitchen paper!

1. Put a **cloth** on the table.

2. If you have **placemats**, put down one placemat for every person, in front of their seat.

3. Put a **fork** on the left-hand side of the place mat and a **knife** on the right-hand side. (If someone is left-handed, you can swap them round.)

4. If you are having pudding, you will need a **spoon** or a **fork**, or both, depending on what you are eating. How runny is it? If it is apple pie and you are having it with custard or cream, you will need a spoon. If it is carrot cake, you will probably just need a fork. The spoon and the fork should go at the top of the placemat. If there is only one, it should face to the left.

5. If you are putting **cups** on the table for drinks, put these at the top right-hand corner of the placemat so people can easily reach for the cup with their right hand.

6. Sometimes it makes sense to put empty **plates** on the table for each person. When you are serving something like lasagne, you can put the whole **dish** in the middle of the table and the lasagne can be served to each person, rather than being put on plates before it gets to the table.

7. If you have **napkins** or kitchen paper, fold them into triangle shapes and put them either under the knife on the right-hand side, or on the plate, or bend the ends around and tuck them into the cups so they stick up like hats.

And there you have it!

breakfast

boiled egg & soldiers

prep   cook

0   5-7

equipment:
- small saucepan
- big spoon
- kitchen timer or clock
- knife
- toaster (or grill)
- slotted spoon
- egg cups
- teaspoons

ingredients:
(serves 2)
- 2 eggs *
- 2 slices of wholemeal bread
- butter for your toast
- Marmite (only if you like it!)

* Store eggs in the fridge, but take them out a while before you boil them so they warm up. This helps stop the shells cracking when they're put into hot water.

When I was growing up, my mum could not afford chocolate eggs for all five of us, but we all had two boiled eggs each on Easter morning and we loved them. We each removed the tops of the eggs in our own way, and the eggshells got everywhere!

1. Half-fill the **saucepan** with cold water. Place on the hob over a high heat and bring to the boil.

Gently lower the **eggs** into the water using a **big spoon** and turn the heat down to a gentle simmer. Cook the **eggs** for 5 minutes for a soft yolk or 7 minutes for a hard yolk. Use the **timer** or **clock** so you don't overcook them.

2. While the **eggs** are cooking, put the **bread** on to toast. When it's ready, **butter** the toast. If you like **Marmite**, spread it on after the **butter**. Cut the toast into strips – these are your soldiers. Don't forget to keep an eye on your **timer**!

3. Lift the **eggs** out of the **saucepan** using a **slotted spoon** and serve in your favourite **egg cups** with the toasted soldiers.

Use a **teaspoon** to bash the top of the **egg**, then slide the **spoon** through the shell and take the top off.

cheesy scrambled eggs

To me, scrambled egg means collecting the eggs from the hen house and dropping them on the way back! Joke – ha ha!

prep

cook

10   10

equipment:

- weighing scales
- tablespoon
- small bowl
- fork
- toaster (or grill)
- small non-stick saucepan
- wooden spoon
- grater

ingredients:

(serves 2)

- 4 eggs
- salt and pepper
- 2 thick slices of wholemeal bread
- 1 tablespoon of butter, and a little extra for your toast
- 40g Parmesan cheese,

1. Weigh the cheese and get your other ingredients ready. Break the **eggs** into a **bowl** and beat well with a **fork** until the **eggs** are completely mixed up. Add a small pinch of **salt and pepper**.

Get your **bread** ready to go in the **toaster** or under the **grill** – but don't put it on just yet.

2. Melt the **butter** on a high heat in the **saucepan** and when it starts to melt, add the beaten **eggs**. Turn the heat down to low. Now start your toast.

Using a **wooden spoon**, stir the **eggs** slowly while they are cooking. The eggs may look a bit lumpy at first but keep stirring!

3. After about 4 minutes the **eggs** should be nearly cooked but still a little runny. Add the grated **Parmesan**. Stir it again, then turn off the heat. You should have a smooth, creamy mass. Don't rush – the trick is to cook the **eggs** slowly and take them off the heat just before they are totally cooked as they will finish cooking once the heat is off. **Butter** your toast and serve with the **eggs**.

nora's yummy eggy bread

prep
5

cook
5

equipment:

- shallow bowl or dish
- tablespoon
- fork
- large non-stick frying pan
- spatula

ingredients:

(serves 2)

- 2 medium eggs
- 1 tablespoon of butter
- 2 thick slices of bread cut diagonally into triangles
- 4 teaspoons of caster sugar

1. Break the **eggs** into a **shallow bowl** or **dish** and beat with a **fork**.

2. Melt the **butter** in the **large non-stick frying pan** over a medium heat. While it is melting, press both sides of the **bread** into the beaten **eggs**. Don't leave the **bread** in the **eggs** too long. If you do, the triangles will get too soggy and they'll break apart when you try to lift them.

3. When the **butter** has melted, use your **spatula** to place the soaked **bread** into the hot **pan**.

This is something I used to make with my children all the time. I think everyone has their own version. Try cutting out different shapes in the bread using cookie cutters before you soak it in the egg, or serve with a little sprinkled cinnamon and fresh berries or sliced bananas.

4. After a couple of minutes, turn the **bread** over – the underside should be golden brown. Repeat until both sides are golden.

Arrange two **bread** triangles on each plate and sprinkle with the **sugar**. Serve immediately.

caramel apple pancakes

prep
(20)

cook
(15)

You can make the batter for the pancakes the night before and leave it covered in the fridge so that you can have a lazy lie-in and not have to prepare it the next morning! You can also make double the amount of batter to make extra pancakes, which you can wrap in clingfilm once they are cooked and keep in the freezer. That way you have them ready to warm up at any time.

equipment:
- **weighing scales**
- **sieve**
- **large bowl**
- **hand whisk**
- **large non-stick frying pan**
- **corer (if you have one, or you can use the small sharp knife)**
- **vegetable peeler (optional)**
- **small sharp knife**
- **chopping board**
- **large saucepan with a lid**
- **small ladle**
- **plastic spatula or metal palette knife**
- **heatproof plate**
- **foil**

ingredients:
(makes about 8 pancakes)
- **50g plain flour**
- **a pinch of salt**
- **150ml milk**
- **1 egg**
- **30g butter, plus 2 more tablespoons for frying**
- **4 medium-size apples – any variety you like**
- **3 heaped tablespoons of honey**
- **maple syrup or extra honey, for drizzling**

caramel apple pancakes

1. Weigh and get ready your ingredients. To make the pancake batter, **sieve** the **flour** and **salt** into a **large bowl**. Make a hole in the middle of the flour, and add the **milk** and the **egg** into the hole. Give it all a good **whisk**. Melt the 30g of **butter** in the **frying pan**, and add it to the mixture. **Whisk** all the ingredients in the **bowl** together until all the lumps disappear. The batter should be smooth and runny. Leave it to sit for at least 15 minutes. Bubbles will start to form in the **bowl** – this is good. Do not mix it up again before you use it.

2. To prepare the **apples**, remove the **apple** core with your **corer**, peel each **apple** and cut into quarters. If you don't have a corer, don't worry, just peel the **apples**, cut each one into quarters and then take out the core with a **small sharp knife** – this is a bit fiddly so you may need some help.

3. Melt 1 tablespoon of **butter** in the **saucepan** over a low heat and add the **apples**. Pour 1 tablespoon of **honey** over and cook on a very low heat with the **lid** on – the steam from the **apples** helps to cook them so don't peek too often or the steam will escape. After 5 minutes, take the **lid** off and add another tablespoon of **honey**. Cook for another 5 minutes, without the **lid**. Stir every so often to stop it sticking to the bottom of the **pan**. The **honey** will thicken and leave the **apples** in a caramel sauce. Turn off the heat and replace the **lid** to keep them warm.

4. Place the **frying pan** with a little bit of the extra **butter** over a medium heat. You need to add a bit of butter to the pan before you cook each pancake so make sue you don't use it all at once! When it has melted, carefully pour a ladleful of the pancake batter into the **frying pan** and tilt the **frying pan** to spread the mix all over the base. Leave for 2–3 minutes or until the underside is light brown.

5. Flip the pancake over with a **spatula** or **palette knife** and cook for a few seconds on the other side. Don't worry if the first pancake breaks as you flip it over; just keep trying. The more you do, the better you will become. The mixture should make about eight pancakes. As you finish each pancake, keep them warm in the oven on a **heatproof plate** and covered with some **foil** while you are cooking the rest. To serve, lay one pancake on a plate and spoon on some of the **apple** mixture. Fold the pancake in half and drizzle with **maple syrup** or **honey**.

power porridge

prep 5

cook 12

equipment:
- **weighing scales**
- **measuring jug**
- **non-stick saucepan**
- **wooden spoon**

ingredients:
(serves 2)
- **300ml milk**
- **300ml water**
- **60g porridge oats – not the instant kind**
- **brown sugar, maple syrup or honey, to serve**
- **fresh fruit, such as strawberries, blueberries or sliced bananas to put on top (optional)**

When I was a child, we had porridge nearly every day for breakfast. Sometimes I longed for cornflakes, but porridge is still my favourite.

1. Weigh and get ready your ingredients. Pour the **milk** and **water** into a **saucepan**, put on a medium heat, add your **oats** and stir with a **wooden spoon**.

2. Keep stirring until it just starts to boil. Turn the heat down and simmer for 10 minutes, stirring occasionally.

Add a bit more **milk** if you like your porridge runny, or cook for a bit longer if you want it thicker. Pour it into bowls and sprinkle with **brown sugar**, **maple syrup** or **honey**. You can top with **fresh fruit** if you like.

pick 'n' mix
morning munch

prep   mix

5   1

equipment:

- **weighing scales**
- **large mixing bowl**
- **spoon**
- **airtight container**

ingredients:

(serves 4)

- **150g porridge oats**
- **150g dried fruit, nuts and seeds**

You can use any combination of the following as long as they add up to 150g. Remember not to use nuts if anyone is allergic to them. You can also make a great big quantity and keep it in an airtight container so it's ready to eat in the morning. It will keep for a week or two, so if you want it every day for breakfast make lots!

dried fruit

- **raisins**
- **sultanas**
- **apricots**
- **currants**
- **dried cherries**
- **dried cranberries**
- **dried blueberries**

seeds

- **pumpkin seeds**
- **sunflower seeds**

nuts

- **hazelnuts**
- **brazil nuts**
- **almonds**
- **walnuts**

When serving, have ready:

fresh fruit such as

- **blueberries**
- **strawberries**
- **sliced banana**
- **raspberries**
- **chopped apple**

milk

honey

Super easy, and you can get creative with the ingredients! I now realise why my rabbit lived so long and had bundles of energy. Instead of always feeling tired, I should have been eating the rabbit mixture.

1. Weigh and get ready your ingredients. Pick 'n' mix your selection of **dried fruit**, **seeds** and/or **nuts** and put them in a **large mixing bowl**. Tip the **oats** on top and mix well with a spoon – or your hands, if you have washed them first!

2. If you're not going to use all of the munch straight away, put the rest into an **airtight container**. It will stay fresh in the container for a couple of weeks.

Put some munch into your favourite cereal bowl, cover with cold **milk** and add some **fresh fruit** on top. Add a little **honey** if you've been extra good!

banana toast

You can have this for breakfast or as a treat. My children used to bring their mates round to play after school and if they wanted a snack, this was perfect – it's so quick and easy to make and even fussy friends love it!

prep 5   cook 5

equipment:

- **tablespoon**
- **teaspoon**
- **small bowl**
- **small knife**
- **toaster (or grill)**

ingredients:

(serves 2)

- **2 tablespoons of soft butter (take your butter out of the fridge early to let it warm up)**
- **2 teaspoons of honey**
- **½ teaspoon of cinnamon**
- **2 bananas**
- **4 slices of brown bread**

1. Mix together the **soft butter**, **honey** and **cinnamon** in a **small bowl** with a **teaspoon**.

2. Peel the **bananas** and cut them into slices with a **small knife**.

3. Toast the **bread** in the **toaster**, or under the **grill**.

4. Spread the sweet **cinnamon butter** mixture onto the hot toast and pile the sliced **bananas** on top. Eat straight away!

pick 'n' mix smoothies, juices & shakes

prep
5

blend
2

equipment:

- **You may be lucky enough to have a juicer at home, but you can use a good blender or food processor to blend ready-made juices with peeled and chopped fruit**
- **measuring jug**

Just one glass of vegetable or fruit juice a day is a tasty way of giving you all sorts of extra energy and vitamins. Try the suggestions on the right, or experiment with different types of fruits. You can even make vegetable juices!

You can use just about any combination of fruit and veg, such as:

fruit

- **apples and pears* (unless you have a juicer, add apple juice from a carton)**
- **bananas**
- **blackberries**
- **blueberries**
- **kiwi**
- **mango**
- **melon**
- **oranges (squeeze them or use orange juice from a carton)**

- **peaches, nectarines, plums or apricots, stones removed**
- **pineapple**
- **pomegranate**
- **raspberries**
- **strawberries**

vegetables & herbs

- **basil**
- **beetroot* (makes your juice go very pink)**
- **carrots***
- **coriander**
- **cucumber***
- **mint**
- **peppers***
- **tomatoes***

* You will need a juicer for these

You can also add cold milk to the fruit when you blend it to make it into a delicious smoothie or shake, and try adding a handful of ice cubes on a hot day.

Try these combinations to start, then have fun inventing your own potions:

strawberry & banana smoothie
ingredients:
(serves 2)

- 3 bananas, peeled and chopped
- 10 strawberries
- 300ml milk

1. There's only one step! Just peel your fruits or vegetables, and remove any stones if necessary. Then blend together and serve in tall glasses.

peach & strawberry smoothie
ingredients:
(serves 2)

- 2 peaches or nectarines, cut in half, stones removed
- 10 strawberries, green parts removed
- 300ml milk

apricot & orange juice
ingredients:
(serves 2)

- 5 fresh apricots, stones removed
- 500ml fresh orange juice

blackberry & apple juice
ingredients:
(serves 2)

- 1 punnet of blackberries
- 500ml fresh apple juice

tropical smoothie
ingredients:
(serves 4)

- 1 pineapple, peeled, cored and chopped into pieces
- 1 mango, peeled and stone removed
- a small bunch of mint

snacks & salads

quick carrot crunch

equipment:

- measuring jug
- weghing scales
- sharp knife
- chopping board
- lemon squeezer
- bowl
- peeler
- grater

ingredients:

(serves 4)

- 1 lemon
- 1 orange
- 100ml olive oil
- 3 large carrots, peeled and grated
- 100g currants
- ½ bunch of fresh mint leaves, chopped
- salt and pepper

This colourful carrot salad is super-fast to make. It's great either for taking on summer picnics or for serving as a side dish with a larger meal.

1. Weigh and measure your ingredients. Cut the **lemon** and **orange** in half, squeeze each half with the lemon squeezer and pour the juice into the **bowl**.

2. Add the **olive oil**, grated **carrots**, **currants** and chopped **mint**. Sprinkle with a bit of **salt and pepper**, mix well and serve.

tuna picnic salad

prep

15

cook

15

When my son Kieran was young, he didn't like the look of a whole fish, but when we made tuna salad he loved it and didn't realise it was actually fish!

equipment:

- weighing scales
- sharp knife
- chopping board
- tablespoon
- small saucepan
- large mixing bowl or large plastic container with a lid
- colander
- oven gloves
- large spoon

ingredients:

(serves 4)

- 300g new potatoes, washed and scrubbed
- salt and pepper
- 400g tinned tuna, drained
- 1 cucumber, chopped into small cubes
- 1 bunch of parsley, leaves chopped
- 1 bunch of spring onions, sliced thinly, including the green bits
- 200g cherry tomatoes, sliced in half
- 6 tablespoons of olive oil
- juice of 1 lemon

1. Weigh and measure your ingredients. If you are using very small **potatoes**, you can use them whole. If they are larger, cut them into halves or quarters. Place them in the **small saucepan** and cover with cold water. Add a pinch of **salt**, place on the hob and turn the heat on high. Once the water is boiling turn the heat down low and simmer for 10–15 minutes or until they are just soft and you are able to push the **knife** easily through to the centre.

2. Drain them in a **colander**, holding it with your **oven gloves**. The steam is very hot so get an adult to help if you need to. Chop up the potatoes into bite-sized chunks.

3. Mix all the other ingredients together in the **large mixing bowl** with the **large spoon**. Add the **potatoes** and give it another big mix. If you are making this in a **container with a lid**, you can put the **lid** on and give it all a great shake to mix it up. Give it a taste to see if it needs a little more **lemon juice** or a little bit of **salt and pepper**.

4. When it is all mixed, serve it up on plates. If you have made this in a **container with lid**, you can take it with you on a picnic! This is really nice with Quick Carrot Crunch on page 56, or you can serve it with your favourite Pick 'n' Mix Super Salad on page 60.

pick 'n' mix super salad

prep

cook

10

0

equipment:

- chopping board
- sharp knife
- grater
- peeler
- salad spinner
  - if you have one
- large bowl

I used to think salads only had lettuce, tomato, cucumber and spring onions. Now I am a lot more adventurous! I could not believe that mixed leaves with a dressing looked and tasted so delicious. Salads are great to pick 'n' mix. There are so many different ingredients to choose from that there is a perfect combination for everyone. Mix up whatever ingredients you like from the list below, or try adding a few of your own, and choose a dressing to go on top (see page 62). You can make the dressings ahead of time and keep them in the fridge so that they're ready when you make your salad. And salads can be served with just about any dinner.

Get your ingredients together, such as:

vegetables

- lettuce – all kinds
- chopped tomatoes
- cherry tomatoes
- chopped cucumber
- sliced mushrooms
- grated carrot
- chopped spring onions
- chopped pepper –
  peppers come in lots
  of beautiful colours
- sweetcorn
- asparagus
- shredded cabbage

- olives, stoned
- spinach
- beans

meat & fish

- tinned & cooked tuna
- chopped, cooked
  chicken
- cooked prawns
- cooked bacon

nuts

- toasted pine nuts
- toasted pecans

herbs

- mint
- basil
- dill

fruit

- orange slices
- chopped apricot or
  nectarine
- chopped apple or pear

cheese

- try any cheese
  you like

1. Prepare your favourite ingredients. Wash and dry your selected **veggies** or **fruit**, and peel, cut or grate them as you choose. Mix them all up in a **large bowl** if you are making a lot, or put them straight onto your plate. Pour your favourite dressing on top and start munching!

super salad dressings

lemon & honey dressing

prep

5

equipment:
- a clean jar with a lid
- tablespoon
- teaspoon
- measuring cups (you could use a tea cup)

ingredients:
(serves 4)
- juice of 1 lemon
- 4 tablespoons of honey
- 1 teaspoon of Dijon mustard
- pinch of salt and pepper
- 1 cup of olive oil

french dressing

prep

5

equipment:
- a clean jar with a lid
- measuring cups (you could use a tea cup)
- teaspoon

ingredients:
(serves 4)
- ²/₃ cup olive oil
- ¹/₃ cup balsamic vinegar
- pinch of salt and pepper
- 1 teaspoon of honey, if necessary

1. Pour the **olive oil** and **vinegar** into the **jar**, add a pinch of **salt and pepper**, screw the **lid** on and shake it up! Taste it to see if you need to add a little more **vinegar** or **salt and pepper**. If it's too sharp, you can add a little **honey**.

1. Put all the ingredients straight into your **jar**, put the **lid** on and shake, shake, shake!

candyfloss dressing

This is a fun, bright pink dressing!

prep

5

equipment:

- **weighing scales**
- **measuring jug**
- **food processor or blender – this is one recipe where it really is much easier to use a gadget, but the results are worth it**

ingredients:

(serves 4)

- **100g cooked beetroot (if you want to use pickled beetroot you don't have to add the vinegar)**
- **100ml natural yoghurt**
- **a splash of red or white wine vinegar – don't worry, it doesn't have any alcohol in it!**
- **pinch of salt and pepper**

1. Using a **food processor** or **blender**, blitz all the ingredients together until they are smooth and creamy. This is a thick dressing, so you'll probably have to spoon it over your salad.

If you have leftover dressing, it can be kept in the **jar** and stored in the fridge for a day or two. Try experimenting with **lemon juice** or different **vinegars** and **oils** to vary the dressing. Just remember to use the same principle of one-third **vinegar** or **lemon juice** to two-thirds **oil**.

chunky tomato & basil soup
with big fat croûtons

prep
(20)

cook
(65)

equipment:

- weighing scales
- sharp knife
- chopping board
- baking tray
- tablespoon
- oven gloves
- measuring jug
- food processor or masher
- large saucepan
- ladle

ingredients:

(serves 4)

- 1kg tomatoes
- 1 onion, peeled
- salt and pepper
- 3 tablespoons of olive oil
- ½ a chicken or vegetable stock cube dissolved in 300ml boiling water
- small loaf of bread (brown or white), unsliced
- large bunch of basil

1. Heat the oven to 200°C/400°F/Gas Mark 6.

Wash the **tomatoes**. Cut the **onion** into quarters and the tomatoes in half and place on the **baking tray**. Sprinkle with **salt and pepper** and 1 tablespoon of **olive oil**.

Using **oven gloves**, place the **baking tray** in the oven and roast for 45 minutes or until everything is soft and slightly brown around the edges.

2. Just before the **onions** and **tomatoes** have finished roasting, make up the stock in the **measuring jug**. Then remove the **baking tray** from the oven with your **oven gloves** but don't turn the oven off yet.

When my kids were small, they used to love playing outside on a cold day and the thought of a steaming bowl of soup always helped to make them come in. The bread croûtons make this soup even more filling. Basil is a wonderful herb – I think it smells fantastic. Tomatoes and basil go really well together, either cooked or raw.

3. Pour the cooked **tomatoes** and **onions** into the **food processor**, add the **stock** and blend until smooth – you may need to do this a bit at a time. If you don't have a **food processor**, you can use a handheld blender in the **saucepan**. Put the finished soup into the **saucepan** over a low heat. While the soup is simmering, clean and dry your **baking tray**.

4. Rip the **bread** into large chunks (the size of a golf ball). Spread them out on the **baking tray** and sprinkle with 2 tablespoons of **olive oil**. Shake them about a bit. Bake in the oven for 10 minutes or until golden brown. Remove from the oven using your **oven gloves** and place the **baking tray** on a heatproof surface to cool. While the croûtons are baking, take the **basil** leaves off the stalks and tear the leaves into small pieces. When the soup is simmering, throw in the torn **basil** and stir it. Serve the soup in bowls with a couple of the croûtons floating on top.

jacket potatoes
with cheesy filling

prep
(15)

cook
(75)

equipment:
- **weighing scales**
- **tablespoon**
- **fork**
- **baking tray**
- **clean cloth or tea towel**
- **oven gloves**
- **sharp knife**
- **large bowl**
- **potato masher or fork**
- **grater**

ingredients:
(serves 4)
- **4 large baking potatoes**
- **50g Cheddar cheese, grated**
- **4 tablespoons of milk**
- **salt and pepper**

1. Turn the oven on to 200°C/ 400°F/ Gas Mark 6.

Get your ingredients ready. Wash the **potatoes**, prick them several times with a **fork** and put them onto a **baking tray**. Do not forget to prick them or they'll explode in the oven, sending hot potato everywhere!

These are great when we go on self-catering holidays. We stick them in the oven while everyone plays football or rounders. When we come back in, we all scoop out our own potatoes and mix up the insides. It gives me a break from cooking a whole meal – ha ha, what a result!

2. When your oven is hot, cook the **potatoes** for 1 hour or until squidgy when you squeeze them. Use a **cloth** when you do this so you don't burn your fingers, or ask an adult to give you a hand.

3. Remove from the oven with your **oven gloves** and leave to cool for several minutes. When they're cool enough to pick up, cut them in half lengthways, then use the **spoon** to scoop out the insides into a **large bowl** . Try to keep the skins intact – you will be using them again in a minute. Leave the oven on.

Mash the **potato** insides in the bowl with a **masher** or **fork**. Add the **cheese**, **milk** and a pinch of **salt and pepper**, mix well and **spoon** the mixture back into the **potato** skins.

4. Put the filled **potato** skins on the **baking tray** and place into the hot oven using your **oven gloves**. Heat through for 15 minutes until the tops are golden brown.

Serve on plates. Eat them on their own for a snack, or serve with some salad if you want them for lunch.

lunch

pick 'n' mix monsterella pizza

Pizza is great fun to make. Kids always love playing with the dough, and the more you play with it, the better it gets. In our family, all four of us always wanted different toppings. Get your dough ready, then pick 'n' mix your favourite toppings. If two of you are sharing, you can do half and half!

prep 45

rise 25

cook 8

equipment:
- weighing scales
- measuring jug
- mixing bowl
- kitchen paper
- clean tea towel or cling film
- baking tray
- oven gloves
- spoon

ingredients for the dough:
(makes one 30cm pizza and serves 2–4)
- **200g strong flour, plus extra for sprinkling**
- **pinch of salt**
- **7g packet easy-bake yeast**
- **175ml warm water**
- **cooking oil**
- **sauce, such as passata (you can buy it in the supermarket) or tomato sauce (see the recipe on page 82)**

Toppings can include ingredients such as:

vegetables
- **sliced peppers**
- **sliced tomatoes**
- **chopped onions**
- **olives (without the stones)**
- **mushrooms**
- **fresh chillies, deseeded and chopped into tiny bits**

herbs – fresh or dried
- **basil (best for pizza!)**
- **oregano**
- **thyme**
- **coriander**

meat and fish
- **pepperoni or salami**
- **anchovies**
- **chopped ham**
- **cooked bacon**

cheese
- **grated cheese, such as Double Gloucester or Cheddar**
- **feta**
- **mozzarella** – I have trouble pronouncing this, do you (motz-a-rel-a)?

You can even try it with pineapple, or anything else you want to experiment with, as long as it's edible...

1. Tip the **flour** into a **mixing bowl** and make a hole in the middle. Add the **salt** and **yeast** on top. Make sure the **water** is warm (if it's too hot or cold, the **dough** won't rise). Pour the **water** into the hole and mix the **flour** and liquid, using your hands, to make a smooth dough. If it's too sticky, add a little more **flour**. If it's too dry, add a little more **water**.

2. Sprinkle a little **flour** over the work surface. Take the dough out of the **mixng bowl** and knead (see the photos above). Remember, the more you knead it, stretch it and play with it, the better the dough gets, so have fun!

With one hand, hold down the end of the dough nearest to you. With the other hand, stretch the dough away from you.

Fold the dough in half, squash it down and start stretching it again.

You may need to keep adding a little **flour** to your work surface to stop the dough from sticking.

72

3. Clean the **mixing bowl** and wipe around the inside with a piece of **kitchen paper** dipped in **cooking oil**. Place the kneaded dough in the **bowl** and cover with a clean **tea towel** or **cling film** and leave the dough to rise and double in size. This will take about 25 minutes.

If you are going to bake the pizza now, pre-heat the oven. Or, you can put it in the fridge overnight at this stage if you want to save it for the following day.

4. Pre-heat the oven to its highest setting and put a large **baking tray** in the oven to get it nice and hot. **Flour** the work surface and flatten out your dough until it is about 30cm round.

5. Using **oven gloves**, take out the hot **baking tray**, place on a heatproof surface (just be careful where you put it), sprinkle the tray with a thin layer of **flour**, and carefully put the dough onto the tray.

Spread over your **sauce**, followed by your favourite **cheese** and pick 'n' mix **toppings**. Pop the pizza into the oven and bake for about 8 minutes. The dough should be crisp and golden and the cheese melted.

mexican madness

If you don't wrap or roll these right, you end up with a mess everywhere, and the madness will come from the grown-ups!

prep (30)

cook (7)

equipment:

- **weighing scales**
- **tablespoon**
- **sharp knife**
- **chopping board**
- **grater**
- **2 mixing bowls**
- **lemon squeezer**
- **baking tray**

ingredients:

(serves 6)

- **1 red onion**
- **1 green chilli, seeds removed**
- **a handful of fresh coriander, chopped**
- **240g Cheddar cheese**
- **3 ripe tomatoes, medium to large**
- **juice of 2 limes**
- **salt and pepper**
- **six 12 x 17cm flour tortillas**

1. Pre-heat the oven to 140°C/275°F/Gas Mark 1.

Get your ingredients ready. Using the **chopping board**, the **small knife** and the **grater**, chop the **onion**, **chilli** and **coriander** and grate the **cheese**. Cut the **tomatoes** in half, then chop into small pieces. Place the tomatoes in a **mixing bowl** with the chopped **onion** and **chilli** and pour over the **lime juice**. Sprinkle with **salt and pepper** and stir to mix up all the flavours. This is your tomato mixture.

2. Mix the **cheese** with the chopped **coriander** in a second **mixing bowl**.

3. Take one **tortilla**, spread the cheese and coriander mix over half of it. Remember to keep enough to spread on the other five tortillas. Spoon some of your tomato mixture on top of the cheese mix.

4. Fold the empty half of the **tortilla** over the filling to make a half-moon shape. Repeat steps 2 and 3 for each of the **tortillas**, until you have six filled tortillas. Put the folded tortillas on a **baking tray** and put in the oven for 7 minutes until the filling has melted. Cut each tortilla in half, then eat them and see how much mess you make (but remember you'll have to clean it up afterwards!).

cauliflower cheese

prep **cook**

10   40

equipment:

- **weighing scales**
- **tablespoon**
- **teaspoon**
- **grater**
- **large saucepan**
- **small saucepan**
- **wooden spoon**
- **hand whisk**
- **sharp knife**
- **chopping board**
- **colander**
- **oven gloves**
- **medium ovenproof baking dish**

ingredients:

(serves 4)

- **100g Cheddar cheese**
- **50g Parmesan cheese**
- **salt and pepper**
- **40g butter**
- **3 tablespoons of plain flour**
- **500ml milk**
- **1 teaspoon of mustard or mustard powder**
- **2 tablespoons of crème fraîche (it's like yoghurt)**
- **1 medium-size cauliflower**

I have two vegetarian friends who join us every year for Christmas dinner, so instead of turkey they have this!

1. Pre-heat the oven to 200°C/ 400°F/Gas Mark 6. Wash the cauliflower. Grate the **Cheddar** and **Parmesan** separately. Put the **large saucepan** of water on to boil. Add a good pinch of **salt** to the water.

Melt the **butter** in the **small saucepan** over a low heat. Add the **flour** and, using your **wooden spoon**, stir well, keeping the heat turned down low – the mixture should start to look like damp sand. This mixture is called a roux (pronounced 'roo').

2. Add the **milk** slowly, still stirring. If there are any lumps, use a **whisk** to beat these out. Bring the sauce up to the boil, then turn down low and allow the sauce to cook for about 5 minutes, stirring all the time until it starts to thicken. You now have a white sauce, also called a bechamel sauce.

Take the sauce off the heat. Add the **mustard**, half the grated **Cheddar cheese**, all the grated **Parmesan** and the **crème fraîche**. Stir well, then add a little **salt and pepper**. Stir, then taste the sauce. Add a bit more **salt and pepper** if you think you need it.

3. Wash the **cauliflower** then use the **sharp knife** and **chopping board** to cut off the stem. Split the core in half so all the small florets fall apart. Add the cut-up **cauliflower** to the salted boiling water and cook for 4 minutes. It is important not to overcook it or it will go mushy.

Drain the cooked **cauliflower** very well in a **colander**. Be careful – the steam will be extremely hot so use your **oven gloves**. You may need help from an adult.

4. After it is fully drained, tip the **cauliflower** into a **medium ovenproof baking dish** and cover with the sauce. Sprinkle the remaining grated **Cheddar cheese** over the top. Place in the pre-heated oven on the middle shelf and bake for 25 minutes or until the top is golden and bubbling.

When finished, remove from the oven with your **oven gloves** and dish up into bowls. You can serve this on its own for a snack, or use it as a side dish with a larger meal such as a Sunday roast (see page 106).

pick 'n' mix
funky burgers

Homemade burgers every once in a while are a special treat. They are much better for you than pre-packed burgers. You can add things like chopped-up onion, herbs or cheese to the meat for different flavours. You can even try this with minced lamb or turkey for something completely different.

equipment:

- sharp knife
- chopping board
- grater
- large mixing bowl
- plate
- metal spatula

ingredients:

(serves 6)

- 6 soft bap rolls
- 1kg minced beef
- salt and pepper
- any topping you want
  (see list)

Extra toppings – whatever you fancy, such as:

vegetables

- sliced tomatoes
- shredded lettuce
- rocket leaves
- chopped red onions
- pickles

cheese

- Cheddar cheese
- Swiss cheese
- blue cheese

sauces

- mustard
- mayonnaise
- tomato relish
- mashed-up avocado

herbs

- basil
- coriander
- mint – nice with minced lamb

1. Slice the **baps** in half, and prepare any **extra toppings** you are using. For example, you can grate the **cheese**, wash and shred the **lettuce**, or slice the **tomatoes** or **onions**.

Turn on the grill.

2. Break up the **mince** in a **large bowl** using your hands. Add a pinch of **salt and pepper**. Take a handful of the mix – enough for one burger. Shape it into a burger, and put it on a plate. Repeat until the mix is used up and all the raw burgers are stacked up on the **plate** ready to be cooked. Don't forget to wash your hands after touching raw meat.

3. Cook the burgers under the grill for 4 minutes on each side, using the **metal spatula** to turn them over. In the summer, try cooking the burgers on a barbecue!

4. When cooked, place a burger on the bottom half of a **bap**, and pick 'n' mix your favourite **toppings**. Put the other half of the **bap** on top, and serve on plates. You can eat this with your hands if you want, but you might have trouble fitting it in to your mouth!

pick 'n' mix
perfect pasta

To cook dried pasta, just follow the instructions on the packet. The packet will also tell you how much to use per person. Pasta is one of the easiest things to cook. Most pasta will cook in about 8-10 minutes. The cooked pasta should have a teeny bit of bite in the middle. Don't overcook or it will go soggy and fall to bits. If you put a little oil in the water while it is boiling, this helps to stop it sticking together.

Once you have chosen which shape you want to cook, try it with one of these sauces. As you get better at making them, you can invent your own. Try adding different herbs or vegetables to the sauce while it is cooking, such as peas or chopped courgettes.

There are so many different kinds of pasta. They come in lots of different shapes and sizes. You can even get them in different colours, like red or green (these are coloured with tomato and spinach). The fun thing about pasta is that you can pick 'n' mix different shapes with different sauces, and never run out of combinations. I'm sure you already know spaghetti, but look for these at your supermarket (just don't ask me to pronounce any of them).

types of pasta

You can see some different shapes in the picture, but also look out for these others in the supermarkets:

- fusilli – these are really twisty
- linguini – like flat spaghetti
- farfalle – they look like bow ties
- radiatore – look like mini radiators

* In Italian, orechiette means 'little ears'.

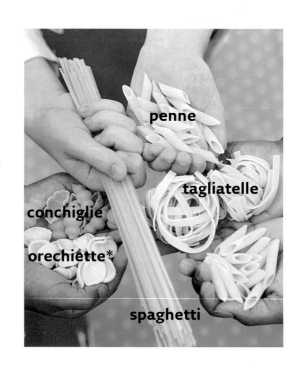

penne

tagliatelle

conchiglie

orechiette*

spaghetti

pesto sauce

Pesto keeps really well in the fridge in an airtight container or spare jar so, if you want to, you can make extra. You can stir it into hot pasta and eat it straight away, or mix it into risotto for a bit of extra flavour. When you stir the pesto into your pasta, you just need enough to make sure each piece of pasta is coated. Make sure you wear an apron and mash and grind gently as this can get messy!

prep
20

cook
0

equipment:
- **weighing scales**
- **tablespoon**
- **measuring jug**
- **pestle and mortar or a bowl with the end of a rolling pin or a food processor**
- **grater**

ingredients:
(serves 2–4)
- **1 large bunch of basil (about 80g)**
- **1 clove garlic, peeled**
- **50g Parmesan cheese, grated**
- **2 tablespoons of pine nuts – do not use if you have a nut allergy**
- **About 150ml olive oil**
- **pinch of salt and pepper**

1. Wash the **basil**, pull the leaves from the stalks and tear them into small pieces. Place in the **pestle and mortar** or the **bowl**.

2. Add the **garlic** and pound it all to mash it up really well. Add the grated **Parmesan** and mash it up again. If you are using **pine nuts**, add these as well and mash.

3. Add the **oil** gradually until you have a thick, green sauce. You may need a little more than 150ml. Add **salt and pepper** then taste.

the quickest **tomato sauce** in the world

prep
(10)

cook
(10)

You can make this sauce while your pasta is cooking – it's so fast and easy. It's a really chunky tomato sauce, much better than shop-bought.

equipment:
- **tablespoon**
- **sharp knife**
- **chopping board**
- **medium frying pan**
- **wooden spoon**

ingredients:

(serves 2)
- 7-8 ripe tomatoes
- 3 tablespoons of olive oil
- 1 clove garlic, peeled and chopped as small as you can
- bunch of fresh basil
- salt and pepper

1. Using the **sharp knife** and the **chopping board**, chop the **tomatoes** into small pieces.

2. Put the **frying pan** on a medium heat and add the **olive oil**. When the oil is hot, turn the heat down slightly and add the chopped **garlic**. Push the garlic around with a **wooden spoon** so it doesn't stick to the **frying pan**. Don't let the **garlic** go too brown.

3. After a few seconds, add the **tomatoes** and cook for a few minutes until the juices mix with the **olive oil**. Stir. Tear the **basil** into small pieces and throw into the sauce at the last minute, then remove from heat. Add a pinch of **salt and pepper**.

bolognaise sauce (also called ragú)

This is my daughter Laura's favourite. She started making this when she was a girl. She's grown up now and she still makes it for her best friends! This takes some time to prepare, so make it before you cook your chosen pasta. Serve it with grated Parmesan cheese on top.

prep **cook**

15 45

equipment:
- tablespoon
- weighing scales
- sharp knife
- chopping board
- measuring jug
- frying pan with a lid
- wooden spoon
- grater

ingredients:
(serves 4-6)
- 1 tablespoon of butter
- 1 carrot
- 1 onion
- 1 stick of celery
- 350g minced beef
- 3 tablespoons of tomato purée
- 1 beef or vegetable stock cube dissolved in 300ml of boiling water
- 400g tin of chopped tomatoes
- salt and pepper
- small block of Parmesan cheese, grated, to serve

1. Get all your ingredients ready. Weigh out the mince. Peel and chop the carrot, onion and stick of celery as small as you can. Heat the **frying pan** over a medium heat and add the **butter**. Then add the chopped **carrot**, **onion** and **celery**, stirring occasionally with a **wooden spoon**. When the veg have softened, add the **minced beef** and stir slowly for 3 minutes.

2. Stir in the **tomato purée** and add 200ml of the **stock** and the **tin of chopped tomatoes**. Add a pinch of **salt and pepper**. Bring to the boil, then turn the heat down to low, put a **lid** on and simmer for 30-40 minutes. This sauce is best cooked slowly. Top with grated Parmesan.

baked macaroni cheese

10 20

equipment:

- weighing scales
- teaspoon
- sharp knife
- chopping board
- large saucepan
- medium saucepan or frying pan
- grater
- large ovenproof baking dish
- colander
- sharp knife
- oven gloves

ingredients:

(serves 4)

- 1 medium onion, peeled
- 120g ham
- handful of parsley
- 350g macaroni
- 1 teaspoon of butter
- 300g crème fraîche (it's like yogurt)
- 250g soft cream cheese
- 60g Parmesan cheese, grated (save a bit for the top)
- salt and pepper

1. Pre-heat the oven to 200°C/ 400°F/Gas Mark 6.

Use the **sharp knife** and **chopping board** to chop the onion, ham and parsley into small bits.

Bring a **large saucepan** of water to boil. Add the **macaroni** to the boiling water, wait for it to boil again, and give it one good stir to keep the **macaroni** from sticking together. Turn the heat down slightly and simmer for 10 minutes. Check it every once in a while to make sure it isn't sticking. If it bubbles over the side, turn the heat down a little more.

2. While the **macaroni** is simmering, melt the **butter** in the **medium saucesan** or **frying pan** over a medium heat. Add the **onion** and fry gently for a few minutes. Be sure to push the **onion** around in the **pan** so it doesn't stick. Turn the heat down to low, and stir in the **crème fraîche**, **cream cheese** and **Parmesan cheese** (keep a little bit of the **Parmesan** aside for later). Keep stirring until all the ingredients have mixed together. Add a pinch of **salt and pepper**.

3. Add the **chopped ham** and **parsley** to the sauce. Mix in well, and then pour the sauce into your **baking dish**.

Macaroni is a hollow tube of pasta which lets the sauce squish about inside. My daughter Laura started making it all by herself when she was 10.

4. When the **macaroni** has finished cooking, drain it very well in a **colander**. Remember, the steam will be very hot! You may need some help from an adult.

5. Stir the **macaroni** into the **baking dish** with the sauce. Make sure it's coated well. Then sprinkle the top with the leftover **Parmesan** – do not mix it in.

Using your **oven gloves**, place the baking dish in the hot oven for 10 minutes.

After about 10 minutes, when the top has turned a golden brown colour, remove the dish from the oven using **oven gloves**, then serve on plates with a side salad or cooked vegetable, such as peas.

sticky messy ribs

Ribs go really well with corn-on-the-cob. That way, you can eat your whole dinner with your fingers and not bother with knives and forks!

equipment:

- garlic crusher (if you have one)
- sharp knife
- chopping board
- teaspoon
- grater
- large plastic freezer bag
- tablespoon
- roasting tray
- foil
- oven gloves

ingredients:

(serves 4)

- **8 pork ribs**
- **3 garlic cloves, crushed either using a crusher or a knife and chopping board**
- **2 teaspoons of paprika**
- **pinch of chilli flakes**
- **8 tablespoons of olive oil**
- **grated skin (zest) of 1 orange and 1 lemon**
- **4 tablespoons of honey**
- **pinch of salt and pepper**

1. Measure out and get all of your ingredients ready (crush or chop the garlic, grate the skin of the orange and lemon).

Put the **pork ribs** into a **large freezer bag** and tip all the other ingredients into the **bag** on top of the **ribs**. Squish the **bag** to make sure all the **ribs** are covered by the sauce. Place the **bag** of **ribs** carefully in the fridge for a minimum of 30 minutes (this lets all that nice flavour soak into the meat).

2. Turn the oven on to 80°C/350°F/ Gas Mark 4. Tip the **ribs** and the sauce onto a **roasting tray** and cover with **foil**. Place in the oven using your **oven gloves** and cook for 40 minutes.

3. After the 40 minutes is up, remove the **foil** and spoon the juices over the ribs. Ask an adult to give you a hand. Turn the heat up to 190°C/ 375°F/Gas Mark 5 and bake for another 40 minutes.

Remove from the oven using your **oven gloves**, dig in and serve with your favourite vegetables or salad. Try pick 'n' mix super salad (see page 60).

dinner

the best lasagne ever

prep **cook**
(30) (40)

equipment:
- weighing scales
- measuring jug
- small saucepan
- wooden spoon
- whisk
- medium or large baking dish
- oven gloves

ingredients:
(serves 6)
- 50g butter
- 50g plain flour
- 850ml milk
- 100g Parmesan or Cheddar cheese, grated
- salt and pepper
- Bolognaise sauce on page 83, or tomato sauce on page 82
- 6 sheets of lasagne pasta (must say 'no pre-cooking required')

This is a simple lasagne and is very easy to prepare. It can be prepared the day before, kept in the fridge and then warmed up, so it's perfect to make for special occasions.

1. Pre-heat the oven to 180°C/ 350°F/Gas Mark 4. Weigh out and get your ingredients ready.

To make the cheese sauce, melt the **butter** in a **small saucepan** over a low heat, add the **plain flour** and stir with your **wooden spoon** until it becomes a light, sandy colour. Gradually add the **milk**, stirring all the time to make a smooth, thick sauce. If you pour in the **milk** too quickly you may end up with lumps. If so, give it a good beat with a **whisk** to break them up. Leave to cook for a couple of minutes, then add half the **cheese** and a little **salt and pepper**.

2. Line the bottom of the **baking dish** with half of the **bolognaise sauce** (or **tomato sauce** for a vegetarian version). Top with a third of the cheese sauce. Do not mix together – you want it to be in layers.

3. Lay half the **pasta sheets** over the sauce in one layer (depending on the size of your **baking dish**). Pour the other half of the **bolognaise sauce** over the **pasta**, then another third of the cheese sauce. Add another layer of pasta sheets, then the rest of the cheese sauce.

4. Sprinkle with the rest of the cheese. Place in the oven using your **oven gloves**. If it's too heavy, ask for help. Bake in the oven for 40 minutes. The sauces should be bubbling and there will be some nice crispy bits. When the lasagne has finished cooking, remove from the oven using your **oven gloves**. Let it sit for a minute. Cut into 8 pieces, and serve on plates with a vegetable, such as quick carrot crunch on page 56.

stir-fry with oodles of noodles

prep

20

cook

15

You can use either dried noodles or fresh, but dried noodles must be cooked and drained following the directions on the packet before you start.

Be careful if you use chillies, because the juices will stay on your fingers and will sting if you rub your eyes or touch anywhere delicate. Wash your hands with soap immediately after cutting or picking up chillies. You can ask an adult to help when chopping them. Taking the seeds out under running water will help.

equipment:

- weighing scales
- teaspoon
- tablespoon
- large bowl to soak dry noodles if you aren't using fresh noodles
- sharp knife
- chopping board
- garlic crusher (optional)
- vegetable peeler
- grater
- wok or frying pan
- wooden spatula

ingredients:

(serves 6)

- 2 cloves garlic, peeled and crushed or chopped as small as you can
- thumb-sized piece of fresh ginger, peeled and grated
- 1 fresh chilli, chopped and seeds removed (optional) – see the note above for hints on handling chillies
- 1 courgette, sliced into strips
- 1 red pepper, seeds removed and sliced into thin strips
- 1 carrot, peeled first, then peeled into strips using the vegetable peeler.
- 125g mushrooms, sliced
- 5 spring onions, sliced
- 125g mange tout
- 4 tablespoons of sesame oil
- 1 teaspoon of curry paste or powder
- 115g beansprouts
- 300g fresh cooked egg noodles or 250g dried – see note above
- 3 tablespoons of water
- 15g pack fresh coriander, chopped
- 2 tablespoons of soy sauce

stir-fry with oodles of noodles

1. Prepare the **garlic**, **ginger**, **chilli**, **courgette**, **pepper**, **carrot**, **mushrooms**, **spring onions** and **mange tout** . Weigh out and get ready the other ingredients.

2. Remember to chop the vegetables to the size given in the ingredients list, to make sure that everything cooks evenly and is ready at the same time.

3. Heat the **wok** or **frying pan** and add the **sesame oil**. When the oil is very hot, add the **garlic**, **ginger** and **chilli** (if you are using it) and stir with your **wooden spatula** for a few seconds. Add the rest of the prepared **vegetables** and **curry paste** or **powder**. Keep on a high heat and fry, stirring all the time. This is stir-frying!

4. After a few minutes add the **beansprouts** and **noodles**.

5. While stirring, add the **water**, **coriander** and **soy sauce**. You may need a little help, especially if you are using a **wok**. Stir well for a couple more minutes. The stir-fry is ready when the **mushrooms** and **peppers** have just wilted or shrivelled.

Serve on plates or in bowls.

big fish pie

Living in the country, our family days out at the river were always fun, especially if someone actually caught some fish for pies.

prep
(20)

cook
(25)

equipment:

- **weighing scales**
- **measuring jug**
- **tablespoon**
- **vegetable peeler**
- **sharp knife**
- **chopping board**
- **2 large saucepans**
- **colander**
- **whisk**
- **large oven-proof dish**
- **grater**
- **oven gloves**

ingredients:

(serves 6)

- **900g potatoes**
- **pinch of salt & pepper**
- **100g butter**
- **50g plain flour**
- **1 vegetable stock cube dissolved in 500ml water**
- **1 heaped tablespoon of crème fraîche**
- **300g salmon & 600g white fish, skinned and cubed**
- **3 tablespoons of fresh parsley**
- **1 bunch spring onions**

1. Weigh out and get ready your ingredients. Peel the **potatoes** with the **vegetable peeler**. Cut any big ones in half. Put them in a **large saucepan**, cover them with cold water, add a big pinch of **salt** and put them on the hob to boil on a high heat. Once they are boiling, turn the heat down slightly, simmer for 10 minutes and then take them off the heat. They will still be a bit hard at this point but don't worry – they will be just right for grating later.

2. Drain the **potatoes** in a **colander**. You may need to wear your **oven gloves** becuase of the hot steam. You may wish to ask for help as the **colander** might be heavy. Leave the **potatoes** to cool for a bit.

3. Pre-heat the oven to 200°C/400°F/Gas Mark 6. Make up the stock in a measuring jug. Melt half the **butter** (50g) on a low heat in the second **large saucepan**. When the **butter** has melted, add the **flour** and stir well. This mixture is called a roux – pronounced 'roo'.

Make sure that any bones are removed from the fish. Tinned salmon works just as well as fresh salmon, and haddock or coley are good types of white fish to use.

4. Use your **whisk** to stir in the **stock** a little bit at a time. Wait until each bit is mixed in well before adding the next bit. When all the liquid has been added, turn the heat up slightly, add the **crème fraîche** and gently whisk again until smooth. Turn off the heat.

5. Chop the parsley. Add the pieces of **fish**, the **parsley** and a pinch of **salt and pepper**. Mix very gently being careful not to break up the **fish** too much. Spoon the **fish** mixture into the **oven-proof dish**. Grate the warm **potatoes** back into the **saucepan**. Sprinkle with a pinch of **salt and pepper** and stir gently.

6. Spoon the grated **potatoes** on top of the **fish** mixture (don't worry if there are a few gaps). Slice the **spring onions** into rings and sprinkle over. Melt the remaining **butter** in a pan or in the microwave and pour evenly over the top, making sure you cover all the **spring onions**. Using your **oven gloves**, place the **oven-proof dish** in the pre-heated oven and cook for 25 minutes. Once cooked, remove from the oven using your **oven gloves**. Serve on plates with a green vegetable such as peas.

pea & bacon risotto

cook
25

equipment:

- **measuring jug**
- **tablespoon**
- **weighing scales**
- **sharp knife**
- **chopping board**
- **2 large saucepans, one with a lid**
- **wooden spoon**
- **ladle**

ingredients:

(serves 6)

- **2 stock cubes dissolved in 2 litres of boiling water**
- **2 tablespoons of olive oil**
- **1 medium onion, peeled and chopped**
- **2 sticks of celery, chopped**
- **200g streaky bacon, chopped into bits**
- **salt and pepper**
- **350g risotto rice**
- **100g Parmesan cheese, grated**
- **200g frozen peas**
- **1 tablespoon of butter**

1. Weigh out and get ready your ingredients. Chop the **onion**, **celery** and **bacon**. Make up the **stock** in a **measuring jug**. Put the **stock** in a **saucepan** on a high heat and bring to a boil. Once it starts boiling, turn the heat down low so that the **stock** simmers gently.

2. While this is simmering, heat the **olive oil** in the other **saucepan** over a medium heat and add the **onion** and **celery**. Stir with your **wooden spoon** and cook until soft but not brown. Add the **bacon** and cook for a few more minutes. Add a pinch of **salt and pepper**.

I wouldn't have had the confidence to try this before I met Jamie. It sounds complicated, but it's really very easy. Once you have learned the basic recipe, you can try it with other ingredients such as courgettes, mushrooms or pesto (see page 81). If you're vegetarian, make it without the bacon.

3. Add the dry **risotto rice** to the **pan** with the **onions** and stir to coat the rice with the oil. Take the lid off the stock. Get somebody to help you add the warm **stock**, a **ladleful** at a time, while you keep stirring slowly. Add more **stock** every few minutes until the **rice** is cooked. This should take about 20 minutes. Keep stirring! The more you stir, the creamier and richer the **rice** gets. Don't put all the **stock** in at once – the **rice** needs to absorb it gradually. When cooked, it should be soft and runny, but not mushy. Add extra **stock** or **water** if it's too dry.

4. When the **rice** is ready, stir in the grated **Parmesan** and the **frozen peas**. You don't need to cook the **peas** first – the heat from the risotto will be enough. Cook for a further couple of minutes, then turn off the heat and put the **lid** on the **large saucepan**. Leave the risotto to sit for about 5 minutes. Stir in the **butter** and serve in bowls.

sausages & mash with gravy

prep
12

cook
30

My mum cooked the best sausages – doesn't everyone's mum? It was a three-mile walk back home from school so it was always lovely to have this waiting for us on a cold day. My family called me 'the dustbin' because I always ate everyone else's leftovers! This is nice to serve with a green vegetable like spinach or broccoli.

equipment:

- tablespoon
- weighing scales
- sharp knife
- chopping board
- vegetable peeler
- large saucepan
- fork
- large frying pan with a lid
- spatula or tongs
- measuring jug
- plate
- wooden spoon
- colander
- potato masher
- spoon

ingredients:

(serves 4-6)

- 3 red onions
- 6 large white potatoes
- salt and pepper
- 12 pork sausages
- 2 tablespoons of oil
- 1 tablespoon of plain flour
- 1 chicken stock cube, dissolved in 500ml water
- 3 tablespoons of balsamic vinegar
- 1 tablespoon of chopped fresh or dried thyme
- 50g butter
- 3 tablespoons of milk

sausages & mash with gravy

1. Pre-heat the oven to 190°C/375°F/Gas Mark 5.

Weigh out the butter and get your other ingredients ready. Peel and chop the **red onions** as small as you can.

Peel the **potatoes** and cut into big chunks. Put them in a **large saucepan** of water on the hob. Add a pinch of **salt**, but do not turn on the heat yet.

Prick the **sausages** with a **fork**. This helps to keep the sausages from splitting when they are cooking.

2. Heat the **oil** in the **frying pan**. Add the **sausages** to the pan and fry them over a medium to low heat until they start to turn brown. After about 3 minutes, use the **spatula** or **tongs** to take the **sausages** out, and keep them to one side on a **plate** while you make your gravy.

3. Make up the stock in a **measuring jug**.

Add the **red onions** to the **frying pan** you've just used for the **sausages** and fry for about 5 minutes, until soft – careful not to burn them! Push them about with a **wooden spoon** to keep them from sticking to the **frying pan**.

After 10 minutes, sprinkle the **flour** over the **red onions** and stir. Cook for another couple of minutes.

4. Slowly add the **stock**, stirring all the time to make a thin onion gravy. Add the **vinegar** and **thyme**, **salt and pepper**. Bring to a boil and stir again.

Take the plate with the sausages on and, using a **spatula** or **tongs**, put them back into the **frying pan** with the gravy. Put the **lid** on and turn the heat down low. Cook for 30 minutes.

While the **sausages** and gravy are cooking, turn the heat on high for your **potatoes**. Bring the water to a boil.

5. After about 20 minutes test the **potatoes** with a **sharp knife**. When they are soft, drain them very well in a **colander**. The steam will be very hot so be careful. You may need help with this.

Once they are drained, put the hot **potatoes** back into the same **saucepan** they came out of.

6. Mash them with your **potato masher**, and add the **butter** and **milk**. Mash well again and add **salt and pepper**. Taste. You can add more milk if they are a bit thick.

Taste a bit of the gravy with a **spoon** (blow on it!), and add a pinch of **salt and pepper** if it needs a bit more.

coriander chicken curry

equipment:

- **tablespoon**
- **teaspoon**
- **2 chopping boards**
- **2 sharp knives**
- **medium/large saucepan or casserole dish with lid**
- **pestle and mortar, or bowl with rolling pin**

ingredients:

(serves 4)

- **2 tablespoons of coriander seeds (or 2 tablespoons of pre-ground)**
- **2 tablespoons of cumin seeds, (or 2 tablespoons of pre-ground)**
- **1 teaspoon of fennel seeds (or ½ teaspoon of pre-ground)**
- **1 tablespoon of butter**
- **1 medium onion**
- **12 chicken thighs, skinned and boned and cut into four pieces each (you can buy them pre-skinned and boned if you prefer)**

- **2 tablespoons of curry paste, such as Madras**
- **1 thumb-sized piece of fresh ginger, peeled and chopped as small as you can**
- **2 x 400g tins chopped tomatoes**
- **salt and black pepper**
- **a handful of fresh coriander, chopped**
- **2 tablespoons of creamed coconut (block form), chopped (you can keep the rest in your fridge in an airtight container)**

My son Kieran has loved curry since he was a little boy. This is a really easy recipe, and he always helped me to make it. Try serving your chicken curry with naan bread, mango chutney and basmati rice, all of which you can find easily at the supermarket.

1. If you are grinding your own **seeds**, do this first so you have them ready. Either grind them in a **pestle and mortar** or in a **bowl** with the end of a **rolling pin**.

2. Peel and chop the onion as small as you can. Melt the **butter** in the **saucepan** over a medium heat. When it has melted, add the **chopped onion** and cook until it softens. Add the cut **chicken thighs**, and fry until the **chicken** changes colour. This will take about 2 minutes on each side, and helps the flavour and to get the cooking going.

While the curry is cooking, you can prepare anything else you wish to serve with it. Warm up naan bread wrapped in foil in a warm oven for 10 minutes, put chutney in a bowl on the table with a serving spoon, and prepare rice following the instructions on the packet.

3. Add the **curry paste**, ground **seeds** and **ginger** to the **saucepan** and stir well. Cook for a few minutes to improve the flavour before adding anything else . Stir in the **chopped tomatoes**. Bring to a simmer, cover with a **lid** and cook on a medium heat for 25 minutes. Keep checking to make sure it does not dry out – add some water if it does. If it is cooking too quickly, turn down the heat a little.

4. After 25 minutes, cut a piece of **chicken thigh** in half. If it is not pink inside, then it is cooked. Get an adult to help you check that it is all fully cooked. Stir in the **coriander** and **creamed coconut** and mix well. Taste with a spoon to check if you need to add **salt and pepper**. Don't burn your tongue! If you are serving the curry with rice, put this in the bowl first with the curry on top.

mum's best sunday roast
with roast potatoes
& green beans

prep
20

cook
60

equipment:

- weighing scales
- tablespoon
- sharp knife
- chopping board
- peeler
- 2 medium saucepans
- 2 roasting trays
- oven gloves
- large colander
- large spoon
- large plate – big enough to put the chicken on when it's cooked
- tongs
- foil
- wooden spoon
- sieve
- 1 small saucepan with lid
- sharp carving knife
- serving plate
- 2 serving dishes
- jug or gravy boat (not a real boat!)

This is a great recipe to get the whole family involved. It's a lot to prepare, so everyone can help washing the veggies, peeling the potatoes, and getting the chicken ready. The trick is to get everything cooked and ready to serve at the same time – once you've learned how to do this you're a roast master! Be sure to read the directions all the way through before you start so you know exactly when you need to put things on to cook. It's also a good idea to set your table before you start cooking so that when everything is done you can take it straight to your hungry family!

ingredients:
(serves 4)

- 2kg potatoes
- salt and pepper
- 100g butter, at room temperature (take it out of the fridge a little while before you need to use it)
- 1.8kg chicken, washed under a cold tap
- 1½ lemons
- 15g fresh thyme or tarragon
- 1 clove of garlic
- 1 chicken stock cube dissolved in 350ml boiling water
- 2 tablespoons of olive oil
- 250g green beans

1. Pre-heat the oven to 200°C/400°F/Gas Mark 6.

Weigh out and get ready your ingredients. Peel and cut the **potatoes** in half if they are small, and into quarters if they are large. Put into a **medium saucepan**, cover with cold water and add a pinch of **salt**. Get them ready to go on the hob, but don't turn on the heat just yet.

Use your hands to smear the **butter** over the **chicken** and put it into a **roasting tray**. If you are using **butter** from a tub or from a larger block, be sure to take out what you need before you start to rub it onto the **chicken** and not to put your hands back into the main tub or block of **butter**. Always remember to wash your hands after touching raw meat!

2. Sprinkle the **chicken** with a pinch of **salt and pepper**. Cut one **lemon** in half and put both halves inside the **chicken** along with the whole bunch of **thyme** or **tarragon** and the **garlic**. Wash your hands very well.

3. Pour the **stock** into the **roasting tray**. Using **oven gloves**, put the **chicken** in the pre-heated oven. If it is too heavy, ask an adult to help you. After it has been cooking for 10 minutes, turn the oven down to 190°C/375°F/Gas Mark 5. The **chicken** will need to cook for a further 50 minutes, but don't run off just yet, there's other work to do.

mum's best sunday roast

4. When your **chicken** has been in the oven for 20 minutes, put the heat on under the **potatoes** and bring to a boil. Once boiling, turn down the heat and simmer for 5 minutes.

Put the **olive oil** into the other **roasting tray**, and using your **oven gloves** place in the oven, near the top, to heat up the **oil**. Get someone to help you.

When the **potatoes** have finished cooking for 5 minutes, drain them in a **large colander** using your **oven gloves**. Shake them around a bit to get them a bit rough. This is the secret to a crunchy roast potato!

5. You will need to get someone to help you remove the hot **tray** of **oil** from the oven. Then, using a **large spoon**, carefully spoon the **potatoes** into your hot **roasting tray**. Be very careful of the hot **olive oil**. Get help again to place the **roasting tray** of **potatoes** back into the oven. After 20 minutes, get help to turn the **potatoes** over and cook for another 20 minutes.

6. After the final 50 minutes are up for the **chicken**, take it out of the oven using your **oven gloves** and put it on a heatproof surface. It will be extremely hot, so ask for help if it's too heavy.

Turn the oven down to 150°C/300°F/Gas Mark 2 to keep your **potatoes** warm. They should be a nice golden brown.

Check the **chicken** is cooked by cutting through the leg. There shouldn't be any red or pink juices – all the juices should be clear and the flesh should not be pink. Get an adult to help you check this.

7. If the **chicken** needs more cooking, place it back into the oven and check every 10 minutes until done. If it's ready, move it onto the **large plate** and, using your **tongs**, remove the **lemons**, **thyme or tarragon** and **garlic** and put them back into the **roasting tray**. Let the **chicken** rest, covered in foil for 15 minutes. Resting the **chicken** helps to improve the flavour and keeps the juices inside.

8. To make the gravy, put the **roasting tray** over a medium heat and use your **wooden spoon** to mush and mix the **lemon** and **thyme or tarragon** into the chicken juices. Make sure you squeeze out the **lemon**, and scrape the bottom of the **roasting tray** to get all those lovely sticky bits.

9. Strain the gravy through a **sieve** into a **small saucepan**, place the **lid** on, and start to warm it up on a low to medium heat.

Put another **medium pan** of water on the hob. Add a pinch of **salt**. Put it on a high heat. You'll add your **beans** to the water in a minute, but not just yet.

mum's best sunday roast

10. Now it's time to carve the **chicken**. You'll probably need to get help with this until you get the hang of it. It may take a little time, so keep an eye on your **green beans**! You'll need to use a **sharp carving knife**, so do not do this without an adult there to watch or help. First, you remove the legs, then the two breasts. Keep slicing until you have enough meat for everyone, putting the meat onto a **separate serving** plate.

11. Your **medium saucepan** of water should be boiling by now so throw in your **green beans**. They will only need 2–3 minutes to cook – be sure not to overcook them!

Using your **oven gloves**, remove the **potatoes** from the oven and put the **roasting tray** on a heatproof surface. They will be extremely hot, so ask for help with this as well. Turn your oven off. Using a **large spoon**, place the **potatoes** onto a piece of kitchen paper to remove any excess fat. Then put them into a **serving dish** and put it on your table.

12. Drain your **green beans** into a **sieve** or **colander**, using your **oven gloves**. Remember, the steam will be very hot, so get help if you need it. Place them into a **serving dish**, squeeze over the remaining ½ **lemon**, and pour a little **olive oil** on top. Sprinkle over a tiny bit of **salt and pepper**, and put the **serving dish** on your table.

Taste the gravy to see if it needs a little bit more **salt and pepper**. Put the gravy into a **jug** or **gravy boat** if you have one and put it on the table. Call everyone in, and enjoy your feast! They'll all be very proud of you.

cakes & puddings

baked fruit

prep **cook**

(5) (40)

equipment:
- **weighing scales**
- **tablespoon**
- **measuring jug**
- **sharp knife**
- **chopping board**
- **large baking dish**
- **oven gloves**

ingredients:
(serves 4)
- **1kg of any fruit with stones, such as apricots, plums, greengages, peaches and nectarines**
- **4 tablespoons of honey, plus extra for serving**
- **570ml water**
- **large tub of natural yoghurt**

If you oven is on and a shelf is spare, baked fruit is easy to prepare, and tastes delicious hot or cold.

1. Pre-heat the oven to 180°C/350°F/Gas Mark 4.

Weigh out your fruit and measure out the other ingredients.

Cut each **fruit** in half, remove the stones and put the **fruit** in a **large baking dish**.

2. Pour the **honey** and **water** over the **fruit**, and place in the oven, uncovered, for 40 minutes.

Remove from oven with your **oven gloves** and spoon into bowls. Serve with a dollop of **natural yoghurt** on top. You could pour a little more **honey** on top for an extra-special sweet treat. You could also cool this overnight in the fridge and serve it cold the next day. Great for breakfast!

zingy lemon cookies

equipment:

- **weighing scales**
- **kitchen paper**
- **large baking tray**
- **greaseproof paper**
- **grater**
- **wooden spoon & mixing bowl**
- **tablespoon**
- **oven gloves**
- **wire cooling rack**
- **spatula**
- **sieve**

ingredients:

(makes about 24 cookies)

- **110g butter (take it out of the fridge early and leave it to soften before using so that it's easier to beat)**
- **a little extra butter for greasing the baking tray**
- **1 lemon**
- **50g caster sugar**
- **150g self-raising flour, plus extra for rolling the cookies**
- **icing sugar**

I think all children like these cookies. Once your lemon is grated, the rest of this recipe is easy peasy. I promise you will love them – they are so tasty.

1. Pre-heat the oven to 190°C/375°C/Gas Mark 5. Weigh out and get ready your ingredients.

Using a piece of **kitchen paper**, smear a little **butter** all over the **large baking tray** so that the cookies do not stick to it once baked. Or, you can cut a piece of **greaseproof paper** to fit into the bottom of the **tray**. Set the **tray** to one side.

Using the side of the **grater** with the smallest holes, grate the skin only from the **lemon**. The grated skin is called the zest.

2. Using a **wooden spoon**, beat the **butter** and **sugar** together in the **mixing bowl** until it is a light and fluffy mixture. Add the **lemon zest** and the **flour** to the **bowl** and mix thoroughly.

3. Put a tiny bit of **flour** on your hands. Take small pieces of the mixture using a **tablespoon**. Then, using your hands, roll each piece into a ball. Place them evenly spaced on the **baking tray**; do not put them right next to one another. Repeat until you have used up all your mixture. Then use your hands to flatten each ball, so it's the thickness of a cookie.

4. Using your **oven gloves**, place the **baking tray** in the oven on the top rack and bake for 5-10 minutes or until the cookies are golden brown. Keep checking them every few minutes while they are baking to make sure they don't overcook. When they have finished, remove the **tray** from the oven with your **oven gloves** and place on a heatproof surface.

Leave the cookies to cool on the **tray** until they start to get firm, and then transfer them with a **spatula** onto a **wire rack** to finish cooling. Remember, the **baking tray** may still be hot.

When they have cooled, sprinkle a little **icing sugar** over the cookies (it is easiest to do this using a **sieve**).

choca-block

equipment:

- weighing scales
- kitchen paper
- 20cm square cake tin or baking dish
- greaseproof paper
- mixing bowl
- electric or hand whisk
- small saucepan
- wooden spoon
- heatproof bowl (or microwave)
- sieve
- rubber spatula
- oven gloves
- wooden cocktail stick

ingredients:

(makes about 10 brownies)

- small amount of butter for greasing tin
- 2 eggs
- 250g caster sugar
- 60g plain chocolate (not milk chocolate), broken into small pieces
- 75g butter
- 90g plain flour
- ½ teaspoon of baking powder
- pinch of salt
- 120g shelled walnuts – do not use if anyone has an allergy to nuts

1. Pre-heat the oven to 190°C/ 375°F/Gas Mark 5. Get your ingredients ready.

Using a piece of kitchen paper, smear butter all over the inside of the cake tin or baking dish to make it easier to get the brownies out once they are cooked. Cut a square of greaseproof paper to fit snugly in the bottom.

2. Break the eggs into a bowl, add the sugar and whisk them together until light and creamy.

This is a wonderful tasty chocolate brownie. A great stand-by for parties as everyone loves it. Make it in advance and it will keep nicely in an airtight tin.

3. Place the broken **chocolate** and the **butter** into a heatproof bowl, set over a saucepan of simmering water, stirring them with a wooden spoon until they melt. Or, you can put the **chocolate** and the **butter** in a heatproof bowl and microwave for 2 minutes on full power, then stir, before microwaving for a further 1 minute.

4. Gently stir the melted **chocolate** into the **egg** mixture.

5. Place the **flour**, **baking powder** and **salt** into the sieve and sift into the chocolatey mixture. Stir very gently, being careful not to over-mix. A rubber spatula is ideal for this. If you are using **walnuts**, stir them in just before it is completely mixed.

6. Pour the mixture into the prepared **tin** or baking dish and spread evenly. Using your oven gloves, place the tin onto the middle rack of the preheated oven and bake for 30-35 minutes. There should be a nice crust on top.

7. Using a wooden cocktail stick, test to make sure the brownies are cooked. Brownies can be a little more moist than a cake, but the stick should still come out pretty clean. Allow to cool in the **tin** for 5 minutes, then cut into squares and tuck in! Warm brownies are lovely with a glass of cold milk.

mighty muffins

prep
(20)

cook
(15)

equipment:

- **weighing scales**
- **small sharp knife**
- **chopping board**
- **muffin paper cases**
- **muffin tins**
- **mixing bowl**
- **wooden spoon**
- **teaspoon**
- **oven gloves**
- **wooden cocktail stick**

ingredients:

(makes 10 muffins)

- **200g plain flour**
- **2 teaspoons of baking powder**
- **50g brown sugar**
- **150ml milk**
- **1 egg**
- **50g butter, at room temperature**
- **4 dried apricots (about 50g), chopped really small**
- **50g raisins**
- **½ teaspoon of vanilla essence**

You can use different fruits to make different flavoured muffins if you don't like apricots. Try chopped-up bananas, currants, sultanas, dried or fresh cherries. Remember you will need 100g of fruits in total.

You can also try apple and cinnamon muffins – you will need 100g of chopped, peeled and cored apples, and you will add half a teaspoon of cinnamon at the same time that you put the flour in the bowl.

how to eat a muffin!

When the muffins are cooked, leave them to cool slightly in the tin for a few minutes. They're best eaten slightly warm.

1. Pre-heat the oven to 220°C/425°F/Gas Mark 7. Put one **paper case** into each hole in the **muffin tin**. If your tin has 12 holes, you can make 12 muffins, but they will be smaller.

2. Chop up your dried fruit using the **small sharp knife** and the **chopping board**. Weigh out and get ready your other ingredients.

Put the **plain flour**, **baking powder** and **brown sugar** in the **mixing bowl**. Add the **milk**, **egg** and **butter**. Stir well with a **wooden spoon** until the mixture is smooth.

3. Add the **chopped apricots**, **raisins** and **vanilla essence** to the mixture, and give it all a good stir until it's mixed in. Try to get lots of air into your mixture when you are stirring so the muffins get nice and big when baking.

4. Spoon the mixture into the **paper cases** so they are three-quarters full. Using **oven gloves**, pop them on the top shelf in the oven and cook for 10–15 minutes. Remove with **oven gloves** and check if they are ready by inserting a **cocktail stick** into a muffin. If it comes out clean, they are ready. If it's wet and sticky, they need a few more minutes.

fruity flapjacks

My kids each had their own flapjack recipes so they could use their favourite dried fruit. They're fun to make, and they leave a mess all over the kitchen (don't tell your parents this!). In our house half the mix was eaten before the flapjacks got into the oven!

equipment:

- **weighing scales**
- **tablespoon**
- **knife**
- **chopping board**
- **kitchen paper**
- **30 x 20cm baking tin**
- **medium saucepan**
- **wooden spoon**
- **oven gloves**
- **spatula or palette knife**

ingredients:

(makes about 12)

- **180g butter & extra for tin**
- **90g muscovado sugar (this is a kind of brown sugar)**
- **6 tablespoons of golden syrup**
- **375g rolled oats**
- **180g dried apricots, chopped into small pieces. Or you can use any dried fruit you fancy such as sultanas, raisins, blueberries, cherries or chopped-up dates**

1. Pre-heat the oven to 180°C/ 350°F/Gas Mark 4. Weigh and measure out your ingredients. Chop up your dried fruit using the **sharp knife** and the **chopping board**. Using a piece of **kitchen paper**, smear a little **butter** all over the inside of the **baking tin** to make it easier to get the cooked flapjacks out.

2. Put the **butter**, **muscavado sugar** and **golden syrup** into a **saucepan** over a low heat and heat gently until the **butter** has melted, stirring gently with the **wooden spoon**.

124

3. Add the **rolled oats**, **dried apricots** or other dried fruit to the **saucepan** and stir well. Spoon the mixture into the **baking tin** and smooth down the top with the **wooden spoon**.

4. Bake the flapjacks in the oven for 18–20 minutes. When cooked, remove from the oven using your **oven gloves** and put the **baking tin** on a heatproof surface. They may still look soft, but will harden as they cool. Using your **sharp knife**, cut the flapjack into 12 squares. Leave to cool and set. When they are completely cool, remove them from the **tin** with either a **palette knife** or a **spatula**.

carrot cake

I love making this any time I have extra carrots. Isn't it funny that you can make a cake with a vegetable?

equipment:

- **tablespoon**
- **weighing scales**
- **measuring jug**
- **teaspoon**
- **20cm square cake tin**
- **greaseproof paper**
- **scissors**
- **sharp knife**
- **chopping board**
- **grater**
- **sieve**
- **large mixing bowl**
- **wooden spoon**
- **plastic spatula**
- **oven gloves**
- **small mixing bowl**
- **wooden cocktail stick**
- **wire cooling rack**
- **palette knife or table knife**

ingredients:

(makes about 12 pieces)

- **3 tablespoons of butter, softened (take your butter out of the fridge early to warm up), plus a little extra for greasing the tin**
- **180g plain flour**
- **pinch of salt**
- **½ tablespoon of baking powder**
- **½ tablespoon of ground cinnamon**
- **200ml corn oil**
- **270g granulated sugar**
- **2 large eggs, beaten**
- **2 teaspoons of vanilla essence**
- **75g carrots, peeled and grated**
- **200g tin of crushed pineapple including juice**
- **100g cream cheese**
- **150g icing sugar**
- **125g shelled walnuts, chopped (save some whole nuts to decorate the top). Do not use if anyone has a nut allergy.**

1. Pre-heat the oven to 190°C/ 350°F/Gas Mark 5. Using a piece of kitchen paper, smear a little **butter** all over the inside of the **square cake tin** to make it easier to get the cake out once it is cooked. Cut a square of **greaseproof paper** to fit snugly in the bottom.

2. Weigh out and get all your ingredients ready. Peel and grate the **carrots**, crack and beat the **eggs**. Put the **flour**, **salt**, **baking powder** and ground **cinnamon** into the **sieve** and sift into your **large mixing bowl**.

3. Add the **corn oil**, **granulated sugar**, beaten **eggs** and **vanilla essence** to this mixture and beat well with your **wooden spoon**. Add the **grated carrot**, **tin of pineapple**, **walnuts** (if using) and mix well. Pour the batter into the **square cake tin**, using the **plastic spatula** to scrape out the **bowl**. Using your **oven gloves**, place the **tin** on the top rack in the preheated oven for 35 minutes.

4. While the cake is cooking, make the icing. Place the **cream cheese**, **butter** and **icing sugar** in the **small mixing bowl**, and beat with a **wooden spoon** until it's nice and creamy.

5. When the cake is cooked, remove from the oven using **oven gloves**. Stick the **cocktail stick** into the centre of the cake – it will come out clean if the cake is ready and the edges will have come away from the sides of the **tin**. If it looks undercooked, put it back in the oven and check after a few minutes. Let it cool in the **tin** for 5-10 minutes, then remove it gently from the **tin** and place on a **wire cooking rack** to finish cooling. You may need help the first time you do this.

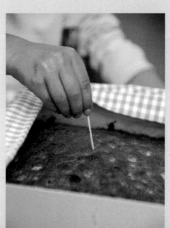

6. Once the cake has cooled completely, spread the icing evenly over the top. If the cake hasn't cooled all the way the icing will melt, so be sure to be nice and patient! If you have a **palette knife**, this makes it a lot easier to spread, but you can use a normal table **knife**. Cut the cake into 12 squares to serve.

fruit crumble

equipment:
- weighing scales
- tablespoon
- sieve
- bowl
- sharp knife
- chopping board
- ovenproof dish
- oven gloves

ingredients:

(serves 4)
- 225g plain flour
- 115g butter, cut into small cubes
- 90g sugar
- 2 big handfuls of Morning Munch (page 48) or oats
- 2 tablespoons of pumpkin seeds
- 1kg fruit with stones, such as plums, peaches or apricots

This reminds me of a trip to the orchard to pick the fruit when my Laura lost her favourite teddy bear. We all had to go back with torches that night to try and find the bear as she wouldn't go to sleep without it. We all enjoyed crumbles as they were so quick, but on that occasion there was no crumble and the teddy bear got the blame.

1. Pre-heat the oven to 190°C/375°F/Gas Mark 5.

Weigh and measure out your ingredients. Sift the **flour** into a **bowl**, add the **butter** and rub the **flour** and **butter** together using your fingers until it looks like breadcrumbs. Add the **sugar**, the **Morning Munch** or **oats** and the **pumpkin seeds**. Mix together with your hands. This is the crumble.

2. Cut all the **fruit** in half and remove the stones – this is easiest using a spoon (see page 17). Place the cut **fruit** into the **ovenproof dish**.

3. Cover the **fruit** with the crumble mixture, but do not mix it in. Place the **ovenproof dish** in the hot oven using the **oven gloves** and bake for 30 minutes. Remove from the oven with your **oven gloves** when it has finished cooking, and serve on plates or in bowls. You can pour a little cream or custard over the top (or even a little vanilla ice cream) if you've been extra good!

pick 'n' mix
rainbow kebabs

equipment:
- sharp knife
- chopping board
- vegetable peeler (optional)
- wooden skewers

ingredients:
(serves 4)
- apples
- bananas
- blueberries
- grapefruit segments
- grapes (seedless)
- kiwi
- pineapple
- peaches
- pears
- mango
- melon
- nectarines
- orange segments
- strawberries, green parts removed
- raspberries

Bet you thought kebabs were only for dinner! You can have lots of fun making these. And who knows, you may even pick 'n' mix fruit you never thought you'd eat before, just to get your rainbow colours right. I'm sure you already know that fruit is full of healthy vitamins, but this recipe shows that it doesn't have to be boring!

1. Choose and prepare your fruit. Cut large fruit such as **apples**, **bananas**, **mango**, **melon** or **pineapple** into bite-sized chunks – peel them or remove the skin if they need it. You can leave fruit like **strawberries** or **grapes** whole. Cut **peaches** and **nectarines** in half and remve the stone. If you are using **oranges** or **satsumas**, peel them and separate the sections without cutting them up. Remember to take care when using your **knife**.

2. Push the **fruit** chunks onto the **wooden skewers**, in any combination you choose. Have fun making different patterns! Serve with one or more of the **pick 'n' mix dipping sauces** opposite.

tropical zippy dip

equipment:
- **sharp knife**
- **chopping board**
- **blender or food processor**

ingredients:
(serves 4)
- **1 pineapple, peeled, cored and chopped into pieces**
- **1 mango, peeled and stone removed**
- **a small bunch of mint**
- **small tub of natural yoghurt**

1. Follow the recipe for the tropical smoothie on page 53, but instead of drinking it out of a glass, put it in a bowl and dip away! You can also try the other smoothie recipes for dip ideas.

yoghurt & honey

equipment:
- **small bowl**
- **spoon**

ingredients:
(serves 4)
- **small tub of natural yoghurt**
- **2 teaspoons of honey**

1. Really easy – just mix it all up in a small bowl. Either put it in the middle of the table for everyone to share, or give each person their own on the side of their plate or in a separate bowl.

raspberry dipple

equipment:
- **fork**
- **bowl**
- **sieve**
- **spoon**

ingredients:
(serves 4)
- **punnet of raspberries**

1. Mash the **raspberries** with the back of a **fork** in a **bowl**. Then push through a **sieve** with a **spoon**. You can try other kinds of berries, or a combination of different berries mashed together.

eat & mess

 prep
(15)

 cook
(0)

equipment:

- **tablespoon**
- **colander**
- **sharp knife**
- **chopping board**
- **large plate**
- **medium mixing bowl**
- **fork**
- **whisk**
- **large spoon or spatula**

ingredients:

(serves 4)

- **2 x 400g punnets of strawberries**
- **2 tablespoons of sugar**
- **284ml carton of double cream**
- **6 meringues – it's ok to cheat a little and use shop-bought meringues**

The famous English public school, Eton, is well-known for this pudding, which they call 'Eton Mess'. This version of the recipe title says it all. Kitchen, floor... sticky mess everywhere! This is a really rich treat for special occasions.

1. Get your ingredients together. Take one punnet of **strawberries** and wash them in a **colander**. Using your **knife** and **chopping board**, take all the green bits off and cut each one in half. Put them onto a **large plate**.

Take the second punnet of **strawberries**, wash them and take the tops off these as well. Put them into the **mixing bowl**, sprinkle the **sugar** on top and mash them up really well with a **fork**. It's ok if they are still lumpy when you've finished mashing them.

2. Add the **cream** to the **bowl** with the mashed **strawberries**, and stir with your **whisk** until it's thick and sloppy.

3. Break the **meringues** with your hands into small pieces and put into the **bowl** with the **strawberry cream**, and add the halved **strawberries** from the **large plate**. Using a **large spoon** or **spatula**, gently mix the whole lot together. Do not mix too much or else the **meringues** will break up too much. You want it to be nice and lumpy.

Spoon into bowls and enjoy!

juicy ice lollies

equipment:

- empty, clean yoghurt pots or ice lolly moulds
- lollipop sticks or small spoons if you don't have lolly moulds
- sharp knife and chopping board if you are adding fresh fruit
- clingfilm or a plastic bag

ingredients:

- any kind of fruit juice (such as apple, orange or cranberry, or mix two different juices together), or cordial mixed with water
- chopped-up fruit, such as apples, berries or pineapple (optional)

It's so nice to come inside on a hot summer's day and eat ice lollies you've made yourself. You can make these with your own homemade juice (see the recipes for smoothies and juices on page 52, but leave out the milk as it splits when it freezes.)

1. Choose your **juice** or mixture of juices and pour straight into the **clean yoghurt pots**. You may even be lucky enough to have proper **ice lolly moulds**. If you are adding **chopped-up fruit**, put this in each container first and then pour the **juice** on top.

2. Place a **lollipop stick** or **spoon** in each **yoghurt pot** or add the tops of the **lolly moulds**. Cover with **clingfilm** or a **plastic bag**. Carefully pop into your freezer and leave for a few hours to freeze up. Be sure to wait long enough so they're properly frozen. When you feel like eating one, remove a lolly from the freezer, take it out of its container and enjoy!

apple pie

This is a great recipe to learn how to make pastry. It's a bit fiddly but just keep trying and you'll get much better with practice.

equipment:

- weighing scales
- tablespoon
- teaspoon
- sieve
- large mixing bowl
- sharp knife
- chopping board
- cling film
- vegetable peeler
- apple corer (if you don't have one you can use a sharp knife)
- rolling pin
- 23 cm round baking dish
- fork
- kitchen towel or pastry brush
- oven gloves

ingredients:
(serves 4)

- 400g plain flour, plus extra for rolling out
- pinch of salt
- 160g butter
- 4 tablespoons cold water
- 3 medium cooking apples
- 4 granny smith apples
- 160g caster sugar, plus extra sugar for sprinkling on top
- 2 teaspoons cinnamon
- small amount of milk for brushing the pastry

mixing the pastry

1. Weigh out and get your ingredients ready.

To make the pastry, sift the **flour** and **salt** into a **large mixing bowl**. Add the **butter**, and using your fingers rub all of it together until it looks a bit like breadcrumbs.

2. When it's all crumbly and ready, sprinkle with the **cold water**. Then use your hands to mix it all together, and then shape the mixture into a ball. You can add a little bit of extra **water** if it's not forming into a ball easily. Don't add too much at a time.

apple pie

3. Wrap the pastry in **cling film** and put into the fridge for 15–20 minutes to help it firm up.

4. Peel the **apples** and remove the core. If you don't have a **corer**, you can cut the **apples** into quarters and then slice out the core with a **sharp knife**. This can be very fiddly, so you may need an adult to help you. Slice the **apples** thinly.

5. Take your pastry dough out of the fridge, and get ready to roll! Clear a big space on a flat surface. Sprinkle **flour** over the surface, and put your pastry ball on it. Using a **rolling pin**, roll the pastry out flat. Turn the whole thing every few rolls – don't turn it over, just turn it around a bit. If you keep turning it while you roll it out, you should end up with a shape that's pretty much a circle. Stop when it's just a little bit bigger than the widest part of your **dish**. You want it to be able to cover the top and have a little bit hanging over the edge. Rolling is a lot of fun, but don't roll it too much or it will get too thin and fall apart or cook too quickly and burn.

6. Put your **baking tin** on top of the rolled out pastry and cut away the excess edges. Use this excess to stick a thin rim around the edge of your **baking dish**. Brush this with a little **cold water**.

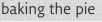

7. Put the sliced apples into the **baking dish**. Sprinkle the 160g of **sugar** and the **cinnamon** over the top of the apples and try to mix it all in.

8. Lay your rolled pastry over the top and pinch the edges down around the edge of the **baking dish** to secure it down. You can cut away any bits that are really hanging down over the side of the dish. With a **fork**, gently make some holes in the pastry so that the steam from the **apples** can escape during cooking.

9. If you wish, you can cut shapes or letters from leftover pastry and lay them on top of the pie. Make sure they're the same thickness as the pie crust, and wipe a bit of water on the back of your shape so that it sticks. If there are any cracks in the pastry, lay the shapes on top to cover up mistakes!

Put the pie in the fridge for 20 minutes for the pastry to rest. This will help stop the pastry shrinking.

Pre-heat the oven to 220°C/ 425°F/Gas Mark 7.

Use a **pastry brush** or the end of a **kitchen towel** to brush the top of the pie with a tiny bit of **milk**. Sprinkle a little **caster sugar** on top.

10. Put in the pre-heated oven and bake for 10 minutes. Keep a close eye on the clock! Then, turn it down to 190°C/375°F/Gas Mark 5 and cook for another 30 minutes until golden on top. Take the pie out of the oven using your **oven gloves**. Serve with ice cream.

139

washing up

We've all helped to make a mess in the kitchen while cooking, so we should all get together to clear the kitchen up and leave it clean. For washing up, get the water nice and warm and put in plenty of washing-up liquid so it's easy to get off all the dirt. If you rinse your dishes in clean water before you dry them, it will remove any soap and help them stay shiny.

Of course, if you are lucky enough to have a dishwasher, you can let it do all the hard work – but remember to load it and switch it on!

index

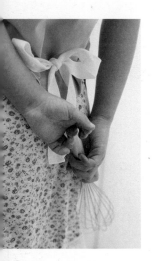

nora's thank you's

A huge thank you to Jamie Oliver. If you hadn't walked into the school kitchen back in 2003, then nobody would be reading this book. I am so grateful for all your help and support.

To Louise Holland for believing I could actually do it – thank you. I truly appreciate all your help. I still can't believe we actually managed to agree on all the recipes! And, of course, thank you to Charlie for testing them with me.

To all the team at Fresh Partners, especially Debbie Catchpole, who was able to decipher all my scribbles and make them into recipes – a big thank you.

To Jenny, Denise and Lisa at HarperCollins. I have really enjoyed doing this book with you and thank you for all your help. Jenny, I hope there are enough carrot recipes for you!

Felicity and Véronique, I had no idea how much time and effort go into getting the right photos. Thank you for all your hard work.

A big thank you to Portia Spooner for all your help.

Thank you to Sarah Schenker

A huge thank you to Greenwich Council and Kidbrooke Secondary School for all your continuing help and support.

And thank you to my husband Tony and my two kids, Laura and Kieran. Sorry for ignoring you all for the last year.

To all the children, thank you for all your help: Clara and Harry Bacon; Bella, Calypso and Jazzi Barnum-Bobb; Adam and Harry Birch; Charlie Colville; Thea Elmsley; James and Kirsty Ford; Emily and Phoebe Fraser; Amy Gruby; Juliette and Charlotte Lassman; Brendan Murphy; Ethan Pack; Iveiana and Kareem Pascal; Latia and Sharna Riddex-Augustin; Brendan and Savannah Ventour; Isobel Warren.

The publishers would like to thank Louise Lawson and Jonathan Swannell for being brave enough to lend us their kitchen.